SUFFERING

BY
ANNE J. TOWNSEND

ARK PUBLISHING
130–134 City Road, London EC1

© Anne J. Townsend 1980

First published 1980

Other books by the same author :

MISSIONARY WITHOUT PRETENDING (FORMERLY ONCE BITTEN)
MARRIAGE WITHOUT PRETENDING
FAMILIES WITHOUT PRETENDING
PRAYER WITHOUT PRETENDING

ISBN 0 85421 886 6

Printed in Great Britain by
Hunt Barnard Printing Ltd., Aylesbury, Bucks.

CONTENTS

Introduction 5

1 Forced to face reality 7

2 Peace not purpose 13

3 Love plus justice 19

4 Identification means suffering 25

5 Hope when helpless 33

6 To lose a child 46

7 To be human – to be hurt 51

8 The joy of pain 57

9 Indifference is easier 67

10 The quality of love is not strained 73

11 The strain of loving 81

12 Strains that threaten to break 87

DEDICATION

Ly Lorn : ex worker with World Vision in Phnom Penh, and new Christian in 1974.

Choeur Sovith : ex Law student in Phnom Penh, and new Christian in 1979.

Im Mealea : ex Law student in Phnom Penh, and new Christian in 1979.

You suffered under the Khmer Rouge, and then lived through the Vietnamese invasion of Cambodia. As you have been forced to flee your beloved homeland may American society offer you peace, security and love.

INTRODUCTION

In the last few years I have read books that told me directly or by implication that to be a Christian is to live a life of undiluted happiness. I experimented with some of the formulae suggested to keep me smiling perpetually. These exercises were a waste of time. I was playing the Greek actor, the hypocrite, who wore a mask to hide his real face.

I have lived in the centre of South East Asia while some of the countries around me fell into Communist hands. I did not smile at the stories I heard from the last missionaries to leave Vietnam. I cannot smile at the heartbreak shared with those who have left Cambodia. I wept with others who left Laos. When I talk with Cambodian and Lao refugees in Thailand, and with the Vietnamese boat people in Hong Kong I find it hard to control my tears.

I have found that Christian joy is more than a bubble of happiness which will burst under pressure. I have learnt of a joy that is strengthened by pain. I have found a joy that persists when happiness is absent.

This book is made up deliberately of pieces of the mosaic of missionary life as I have known it for the last few years. It is not intended to be a complete treatise. Because suffering, bereavement and loving have all been parts of that mosaic I have shared only facets of truth which have become fresh and relevant in my life recently. This book is not a 'complete do-it-yourself' manual.

This mosaic is a fragment of a life. This life is incomplete. It is part of that secret self which is hard to share, yet could be selfish to hide. So these fragments of a life are shared with the longing that through them we shall grow richer and stronger in our relationship with the God we know through Jesus Christ. The God who became man and knows what it means to be human and to suffer.

ANNE J. TOWNSEND, DECEMBER 1979

CHAPTER ONE

Forced to face reality

F ROM the outside the newspaper looked like any other daily paper. The front page stories and photos were ordinary enough.

The story inside of a road accident in Thailand would normally have been read quickly. Yet I could not shift my gaze from that report. All those involved had been my friends. Some had been killed.

In the past living and being human seemed relatively simple. Suffering and loss were events that happened to other people. They did not involve me, and so I could view what was going on from a detached distance. I read books with titles like *The Problem of Suffering* as an intellectual exercise.

In his gentleness God allowed me to face life's realities gradually. He allowed many years to pass before I even sensed the pain that life brings to some.

Perhaps the first events to disturb the serenity of my life as a new wife and mother occurred about twenty years ago. A single woman, and later a married man, both missionaries, were murdered in the hills of North Thailand. The motive for murder apparently was theft of possessions as petty as watch, ring and camera. Surely life was worth more than this? At that time my husband and I were preparing to be missionaries. These deaths added depth to my awareness that God wanted us to serve him overseas. I felt that possibly our two lives might be used in some way to replace those lost. It was a comfort to be able to do something.

This was our first encounter with death. As the years passed death became a recurring and inexplicable theme in the midst of life.

We had lived in Thailand for only a few months when a gifted young missionary died unexpectedly of infective hepatitis. Her death shocked us. We took the simple path of refusing to think about what had happened. Then the following year a physiotherapist who had trained as a new missionary with us was sent home from Thailand to die from a severe neurological disease. She was far away. It was easy to forget her. To think about her was to face questions that disturbed me.

We were busy. Life was for living. At that stage death was a denial of the life of human activity in which we were submerged. Our next encounter with death however was inescapable. A new missionary paediatrician had just completed her year of initial Thai language study in Bangkok. She was ready to start work at Manorom hospital. She diagnosed her own disease long before she shared the news with the rest of us. We hoped her diagnosis was wrong. Surgery proved her fears to be correct. She had inoperable, widespread cancer. She was flown back to be treated and ultimately to die in her home country, Ireland.

Her illness hit me hard. I happened to be staying at the old OMF headquarters in London when she returned from Thailand. I remembered the radiant young woman I had left in Bangkok earlier when I went on leave. She was longing to begin her work at Manorom hospital. She felt that her whole life culminated in this calling. Now her life's purpose seemed to have been cut off before it had even begun.

I had to go shopping for her to buy some clothes that would fit round her distended waist. She was too weak to cope with shopping in London's rush-hour. Her tropical clothes were too thin for the autumn frost. In the impersonal vastness of a West End store I realised that the only clothes that I could find that would fit her were maternity dresses. The shop assistant seeing my misty eyes and reluctance to buy anything listened with concern to my story. She cut off all the labels like 'Mother's Joy' and 'Baby Delight' as I bought and took away dresses designed for one carrying a new life to give a young woman to wear in the terminal months of hers.

I could no longer stand apart and view suffering and death objectively. My emotions began to force my intellect to question. I could not accept such a death apathetically. Whether I liked it or not I was now involved.

My children grew from babies to toddlers and danced the days away to the tune only children hear. As months of their lives passed I heard a distant drum beat rolling to a climax for death's music occasionally muffled the children's dance tune.

A friend was killed in a road accident in Thailand. She had been someone to whom I could flee on a day off with my young children and have fun. In the intensity of trying to be a model new missionary this older missionary taught me how to laugh. Above all, she taught me to laugh at myself. I had known her since I was a schoolgirl. She was a friend of my parents. So she had spelled security and a link with home to me when I was an insecure new missionary. Her sudden death trapped me in a net of emotional involvement. I could no longer watch what was happening as if I was in the audience of a play. I began to feel that some role was required of me on the stage as an actor in life's inexplicable drama.

Life continued as usual. And yet the inexplicable thread of bereavement ran throughout the life that I was so busy living. A few years later two OMF missionary nurses were taken hostage, and then murdered by bandits in South Thailand. In the north of Thailand a missionary father was killed. Later, news spread through the OMF family that a missionary wife had died unexpectedly of cancer while on holiday in England, visiting her new grandchild. I had known them all.

God did not allow me to evade unpleasant issues any more. The biggest blow came when five adult missionaries, seven children (and three full-term unborn babies), most of whom were close friends of mine, were killed at Manorom in a road accident in 1978.

Fifteen adult missionaries and seven children belonging to the OMF family in Thailand died in 18 years. I belong to that family too.

As a child my life had been easy. I knew where I was with my parents. I trusted that my father was both strong enough and loving enough to stop anything bad from happening to me.

When I was little I was bullied by big, ten-year-old boys on my way home from school. I told my parents. The next day my mother followed me home, caught the boys, and ended their cruel teasing. It did not enter my head that my parents might be powerless to intervene, nor that they would ever be indifferent to a small girl's misery.

When I became an adult, I transferred my sense of security

in my human father to God. The Bible seemed to back up my instinctive attitude towards God. From it, I learned of a Heavenly Father who was also the Almighty Creator God. He made the world and was still active in his creation. I had no doubts that God was powerful enough to change anything in the world if he wanted to. I was certain of another feature about God. I was confident that he was perfectly good and loving. I did not believe that he ever acted out of any motive other than supreme love.

However, these two basic truths about God's nature were shaken as I grew older. Life forced questions into a mind that had been quiescent and accepting. Unresolved questions threatened to rip my faith to shreds. I looked at the world around me. While I looked long and hard I bought maternity dresses for a girl facing death from the malignant life within her. Perplexity at times led to rebellion.

'Can a God of love allow this?'

'Has God, who is love, become impotent, so that he is powerless to intervene?'

'Is God powerful, but indifferent?'

If I could find no traces of God's goodness and power in events, then perhaps my faith needed radical re-evaluation. I was trying to take Christianity seriously and not to play a game of being a Christian. A foundation of my faith was belief in a God, who not only is good, but also is all-powerful.

Perplexing events in the world around me and in my own life made me seek even the shadow of God's love and power, as reassurance that my faith was not based on false foundations. If I could have rested under only the shadow of such a rock, then I would have been reassured, yet sometimes shadows seemed too like illusions. I was left at times with neither rock nor shadow in a bleak desert where faith faltered.

I began seriously to question whether God's power was limited. How could a God who was good tolerate the terrible things that were happening? A simple answer might be that such matters were beyond his control. He was not all-powerful. Yet this concept of God did not fit in with the God of Christianity, as I had encountered him in the Bible. Another way round the problem would be to state that God did not prevent bad events because he did not see them as wrong. In other words, I would be claiming that God is not good.

If my parents had left me as a child to the mercy of the bullies who teased me on the way home from school, then I could have deduced that they thought there was nothing wrong in my being bullied, or that they did not care, or that they were powerless to stop me from being hurt. I realised that I could react similarly to God when I saw wrong happening in his world. I deliberately had to exercise faith to believe that God is both good and also all-powerful when life's events appeared to proclaim that this was not so.

Such faith does not mean total abandonment of intellect, although it may call for postponement in drawing conclusions. It does mean that questioning is best carried out when I am emotionally secure and can inwardly trust that, contrary to external factors, God personifies love and omnipotence. Such inward security gives me the serenity and freedom to question safely.

Job is a man who was commended by God for voicing his doubts about him. He experienced suffering in many aspects, yet rested securely in his certainty of God's goodness. His questions arose from the profound perplexity of a man who is good. He freely questions God's actions when God appears to be unjust. Deep security in God's goodness may give us the liberty to think through problems when life forces them on us. We need not ignore or evade these issues. However, some of us are not always secure enough in God to be able to face such questions. Bereavement or tragedy may shake us deeply, turning our feelings upside-down. Our spiritual nature is bound up with our emotions. Until we can cope emotionally we may be unable to handle the spiritual turmoil which sometimes accompanies psychological disquiet. If this happens, then we are right to allow emotional wounds to heal and to shelve our spiritual perplexity. Later we will be able to think clearly without emotions blurring our thoughts. We need not pile spiritual distress on to mental upheavals. Therefore some of us should avoid thinking through certain issues until we are at peace within ourselves. Time's healing restores emotional resources for most of us – but 'time' may be weeks or many years.

The deep security of knowing that God is good and loving may return slowly once it has disappeared. To walk in faith without such God-given assurance is to walk as one who is blind, who must trust others to lead him along the right paths. Precipitous intellectual decisions made at moments of crisis, or slow reasoning under prolonged stress, may lead into spiritual wastelands. We are unable to exercise our intellect clearly under such conditions.

I speak from the experience of the past few years which seem to be bitter and barren. These experiences did bear fruit, but only after I had felt that all was lost.

CHAPTER TWO

Peace not purpose

THE notebook fell onto the floor with a thud that jerked me out of the inner world into which I had receded.

I picked it up with heavy heart. I felt as if my hands cupped a country and its suffering people. This was symbolised by the names listed in that book. It was just an ordinary school notebook but the contents were a reminder of tragic events. Events which had been described as more terrible than the holocaust of Hitler's regime.

That book contained the names of 160 Cambodian Christians, known and loved by a friend of mine who had served as a missionary in Cambodia. By the side of only ten of those names was a record of their situation at the end of 1978. A few were in Thailand, some in France, some in Canada.

'What about the other 150?' I questioned him.

A flicker of grief crossed a face that is usually impassive and calm, 'We don't know,' was the brief reply.

'Are they still alive?' I had to know.

He shrugged his shoulders, frowned, and quietly ventured, 'I believe some are . . . ' His voice forbade further questions, for I sensed he might know more than he dared to share.

I held that book with awe. I desired to enfold the people on that list of names with prayer. My cupped hands holding this book were symbolic of past hours already spent in prayer for them.

I turned to my friend, 'Help us never to see these people as statistics. Make us see them as real people. They were your friends. Help us to know them too, so that we shall never forget and will go on caring.'

I needed to see that list of names at that particular time. By the end of 1978 I was becoming thick-skinned and almost uncaring about the events in Cambodia. Several years earlier

I had been grieved and hurt by the fall of that land, and the tragic destiny of its people. I had felt for this race as terror struck them under the brutal Khmer Rouge regime. Yet, towards the end of 1978, when life in Cambodia seemed to be getting worse instead of better, I found I dared not allow my emotions free reign. I could no longer permit myself to feel as deeply as I had done for this land and for these people. My heart was slowly breaking. Thai newspaper reports indicated that things were getting worse and worse, and all I could do was switch off to the situation. To survive emotionally, I had to become mentally deaf to the cry of Cambodia, and blind to its plight. I did not know then that by 1979 the Vietnamese would have invaded that land, bringing unimaginable suffering to the human remnant. Nor did I know that on the eve of 1980, famine was threatening the survival of those who remained. Quite apart from the pain of grieving for these people, I was beginning to wonder if I was a stupid fool for believing that a God like the God proclaimed by Christianity existed in the face of the brutality and suffering I saw. Instead of stopping it, God seemed to allow things to go from bad to worse. What terrible climax could be coming?

I was beginning to require an urgent answer to my shelved question, 'Why God? Why do you allow this?'

I had shelved such questions for several years. I could no longer do so.

I had to find some kind of answer. If God permitted any suffering, then surely, I reasoned, there must be a point to it. I was going to seek sense and reason even if it took me my entire lifetime to find some solution.

It would be nice, neat, and tidy to encounter suffering, and then to be able to claim, 'God allowed this so that the following things could happen . . . ' and reel off a list of clear reasons. The end would clearly justify the means.

If only reality was as simple as this! I longed to find out the reasons, but reasons were usually hidden from me. If only I could actually see as a result of the death of a friend in an accident, that the posthumous publication of his diary had deeply influenced men and women, and enriched them spiritually, then possibly I might be able to justify his death with the words, 'He died that through his writing many would encounter God more deeply.'

His death, and the tragic bereavement of his family and

14

friends, would then not be in vain. A good end would be found to justify sad means.

I wanted to know why God allowed life to be bitter and difficult for some people. I wanted to see visible, tangible results which proved definitely that the gain was worth the tremendous price paid.

Whenever a missionary died, then my heart whispered words about a grain of wheat falling into the ground in order ultimately to bear fruit. I found these words about grains of wheat in the Bible. Being very human I was comforted to take them to mean that I could expect fruit which would satisfy my intellect as being worthy of the sacrifice paid. In practice I was rarely allowed to see fruit which satisfied *me* as being worth the price paid in terms of human suffering.

Sometimes, I thought I saw the opposite. A price was being paid and the result appeared to me to be destruction, chaos and sadness. What kind of fruit was this? In practice for many of us this is the point at which faith and intellect have to meet and join together. Intellect is confounded. We are baffled and bewildered, seeing no meaning in the events around us. Here faith may soar above intellect. Faith can gradually take control of our confused minds, allowing us to believe things which seem beyond human reason. Some of us may need to cling tightly on to God in these times in the absence of any reassuring feelings of faith.

At the end of 1978 I sat talking for hours about Cambodia with another friend who had worked in the country. His love for that race had been infectious, so that through him I too had loved its people. As he shared stories of those escaping as refugees to seek life in a new country, I felt compelled to question him, 'What do such refugee Christians feel about any God who allows such things to happen to them?'

His reply was like an axe felling my tree of questions with its single, simple blow, 'They don't look at it that way. They see the God of love who has brought them out of Cambodia. They experience hope that eventually a third country will welcome them. They only speak of the love of God who has brought them out alive.'

My questions were silenced. Apparently, those who had suffered intolerably did not ask my question, 'Why?'

Perhaps I should no longer ask such a question.

Possibly I should have learned this already, for God had

15

spoken to me in another situation at the beginning of 1978 when I had asked the question, 'Why?'

The swirling greys of Turner's picture caught me up in their emotional turmoil. I was fascinated that an artist should strap himself to the mast of a small sailing vessel in a storm and later depict his *feelings* on canvas. I felt with him in his apparent desperation, lostness and meaninglessness. I glimpsed the pin-point light in the storm that offered possible hope. I sensed the loneliness of his struggle for survival. Did he wonder if the light would fade away or be extinguished?

In January 1978 I paid my first visit to the Tate gallery. I wrenched myself away from the magnetism of Turner's picture and reluctantly returned home to less appealing domesticity.

Yet four days later I was plunged into the reality of Turner's painting. We were spending an unusually quiet Saturday afternoon as a family at home, on leave from Thailand. The telephone rang. Following that call we sat numbly in the kitchen which suddenly seemed cold. An afternoon of happiness turned to grief.

Reality was too immense to comprehend. Could it be true that five adult missionary friends and seven children had been killed in a road accident near our Thailand home, 9,000 miles away from us in England? We had left them alive, and I imagined them as I last saw them. I could hardly believe that five out of the eight missionary families at Manorom hospital in Thailand had been bereaved. Two families had been totally wiped out, another had lost mother and two children, and two others had each lost a child.

The decision that my husband must return immediately to Thailand and assume his role as medical superintendent at the community that was family to us, was natural and spontaneous.

Exhaustion entwined with incomprehensible loss forbade sleep. The following day seemed to be spent in tears or answering the ceaseless ring of the telephone. A Sunday filled by telephone enquiries asking for information, and the repeated recitation of the same story gradually forced the grim reality home. What had happened was real and true.

On 'Children's Day' in Thailand in 1978, several missionary families and children visited a neighbouring town to watch Thai labourers pouring golden rice grains from baskets into heaps to be loaded on to rice barges for export. The midday sun beat down on the children, all aged under seven, running to and fro in delight on the river bank. Saturday outings like this were as rare as they were precious. Then the little ones climbed hungrily into the hospital's Toyota van, ready for the lunch of rice and Thai curries that was waiting for them at home. As the van swung off the main Asian highway, an Australian surgeon called out to the driver, 'That was a beaut day out!'

The driver casually commented, 'We're not home yet!'

His words were too true. Twelve in the van were to enter a totally new home that day.

A few seconds later, his foot automatically slammed down on the van's brakes. A large vehicle was unexpectedly overtaking a stationary bus on the other side of the road and was aimed straight at the hospital van. Head-on collision was inevitable. Twelve people in the hospital van were killed instantly, only two adults and three children survived.

Repetition of this story over the telephone made reality unbearable. It hurt to imagine the gardens at Manorom now silent and devoid of the children running around playing. Nights were haunted by thoughts of empty houses and vacant beds.

Zechariah's words about the New Jerusalem, 'The city streets will be filled with boys and girls playing there' (Zechariah 8:5) seemed a remote promise. I wanted those children and their parents here and now, not there and later.

The loss was impossible to grasp.

Turner's picture gripped my imagination with its restless, swirling currents. My mind raced with different thoughts chasing one another in furious agony. The helpless mess of the situation confused the purity of grief. Where was God? Turner saw light in his picture, I saw nothing but the fury of the storm.

I could identify with the writer of Psalm 77, for his cry to God in deep personal sorrow was mine, 'my soul refused to be comforted . . . my spirit grew faint. You kept my eyes from closing . . . ' I reached for God and could not find him. My prayer was wordless weeping, bringing the hurt in my heart to God.

I had always been assured that in trouble I could rely on

God to be near to comfort me. Yet now I could not sense his reality.

Doubt whispered in the back of my mind, 'Perhaps God doesn't really care. Perhaps you are being deluded into thinking he does, and deluded in believing that he can control his created universe.'

If God was not all I had believed him to be, then this was greater than all griefs. To lose God now was more than I felt I could bear.

In the middle of the confusion came a steady inner directive, 'Be still, and know that I am God.'

I looked again at Turner's picture, and saw now his small, steady light. All I could do in this desolation was to command myself, 'Stop all this! Stop asking these questions! Accept what is happening and see what it can do in your life. You won't find a simple answer to this.'

We want answers. We are geared to a life in which we work and see results of our work. Yet as we face suffering we are rarely allowed to see why God has allowed such things to happen. We are rarely shown the results.

It is hard to accept that intellectually we are not going to be satisfied. Our question, 'Why?' may never receive an answer that is completely satisfying. Therefore we belittle God if we try to work out answers for him and try to justify his actions to others.

God can do that for himself and does not need us to try to explain to others. We are as likely to be wrong as right in this, for we must admit that we are incapable of seeing the complexity of God's purposes.

We forget too easily that we think and speak in the framework of human time, while God's purposes are carried out in another dimension, eternity.

Perhaps we should rest here uttering the simple words, 'My Father, I do not understand you, but I trust you.'

CHAPTER THREE

Love plus justice

With a great deal of pretending I can persuade myself that, unlike some other people, I have lived a perfect life.

'Look at what you've done!' I am tempted to turn up my nose at the first two humans mentioned in the Bible, 'I wouldn't have disobeyed God like you!'

In moments of arrogance I am annoyed that their attitudes and actions have involved me in the consequences of what they did. It seems totally unfair.

Once I've stopped pretending I'm perfect, I know very well that had I been them, I would probably have done exactly the same thing.

Adam and Eve were a privileged couple. They knew that God loved them. He had given them one another and matched them perfectly. He had put them in an ideal place in which to live. Life was as good as it could be. God had commanded them to obey him. There was only one command to keep, and it was hardly difficult. At the same time they were given the freedom to choose whether or not they would obey. Disobedience would be punished. They understood this.

Faced with a growing desire for the only thing God had forbidden them, they gave in. Afterwards God heard their feeble excuses. Their words were little more than buck-passing. The buck ultimately being stopped on God's desk, with Adam's words, 'The woman you put here with me – she gave me some fruit from the tree, and I ate it' (Genesis 3:12).

The God who loved this couple is a God in whose nature two characteristics interlock. He is not only the God of love, but he is also the God of justice. Flagrant disobedience of God's commands warrants just punishment by God.

Adam and Eve received the bitter repercussions of their disobedience. The jolting disharmony they introduced into the world is passed on to us today. The consequences of mankind turning his back on God is depicted in a passage in the New Testament as the agony of a long painful childbirth, 'We know that the whole creation has been groaning as in the pains of childbirth right up to the present time . . .' (Romans 8:22).

Man had been given the world in stewardship by the Creator. Man's relationship with the world is summed up by God's word of command, 'Be fruitful and multiply,' 'Fill the earth and subdue it,' and 'Have dominion over . . . every living thing' (extracts from Genesis 1:28).

If man had acted in God's way then our world would have been a very different place from the world of today. I am generally unimpressed by the way in which mankind is taking care of the world (I cannot claim that I would do any better, given sole responsibility). Phrases like 'depleting resources', 'unequal distribution of wealth', 'rich get richer, poor get poorer', 'millions of dollars for space race', 'drought, famine, starvation, death', 'pollution', and 'remember Auschwitz' characterise, for me, man's caretaker role of the world. Of course these phrases are modified by snatches of the news today, 'smallpox eradicated', 'the "Plant a Tree" campaign', and 'Heads of State agree to send emergency aid'.

When mankind first acted in independent disobedience to God he set the pattern which the rest of us usually have followed throughout the centuries. Our actions have caused much of the mess in the world around us.

We are probably no better, and no worse than our predecessors. We do not seem to learn from past mistakes, and we tend to allow patterns of evil to be repeated.

We know that God's love for us is unshakeable. We know that God's justice is unchanging. We carry the consequences for our corporate and individual disobedience to God in that we reap what we sow. If *we* do not gather the harvest of good or evil ourselves then *others* do.

To be loved, and to be justly punished by the God who loves is a mystery we can begin to comprehend only at one place. At Golgotha our understanding deepens, 'For God so loved the world that he gave his only Son . . . that the world might be saved through him. He who believes in him is not condemned; he who does not believe is condemned already . . .' (see John 3. 16-18). The loving justice of God sent the only Son of God to the supreme act of love and justice on a wooden cross at Calvary.

Until we have had to act justly ourselves, and thus hurt someone we love, we may fail to glimpse even a shadow of God's relationship with us. It is mirrored sometimes in our human relationships.

I have a diary record of a few years ago, written in Thailand, which helps me to understand a little more that just dealings with those we love may be painful to us as well as to others. It describes an episode in which it was necessary to sack an employee.

'All has gone as planned. At 9 p.m. last night John slipped into the locked office to see if the man had hidden a gun inside his desk. He found a small dagger which he removed.

'I woke exhausted. Most of the night I had tossed in the heat of a tropical Thai hot season night. I could not stop thinking of all the things that might happen when the man is sacked. At the worst everyone might strike or certain key staff members walk out. Were things bad enough for this? Imagination raced. As I lay awake on a moonless night anything seemed more possible than it does in the glaring sunlight of tropical daytime.

'I am scared of being left by myself in our wooden house after the man has been sacked. I am afraid for our safety. Could revenge be taken out on us? I now dread John being called out at night to treat a patient in case he does not return. This is a sickening fear of the unknown.

'The sort of thing that was worrying me occurred the other night. John was on call for emergencies and could not be found anywhere for the best part of an hour. Another doctor had to cope instead of him. After 45 minutes of the 'phone ringing repeatedly, asking whether John was home yet or not, I imagined him shot or knifed, dead or wounded in a ditch by the rice fields near the hospital. I did not dare go and search, leaving my son asleep alone. In the end John appeared. He was surprised at the fuss. The explanation was so simple that later I had to laugh. He had been searching for a patient's notes. It had not occurred to him to tell anyone where he could be found, nor had anyone thought of looking for him there.

'I woke frightened of the future. If God really is in control, as I must trust him to be, then can I believe he will calm me emotionally? Never having been in a similar situation before, I have no past experience to record the reassurance that God can help in this area of life. But I prayed that God would control my emotions. Since then I have lost the fear for the future which enveloped me before. If I am experiencing the "perfect love that casteth out fear" then it is remarkable. I now feel quietly peaceful about the future. If this is the "peace that passeth understanding" then I can endorse the fact that it *is* beyond human comprehension. I should be scared stiff. I am not. Yet nothing has changed outwardly.

'The other day even optimistic John was apprehensive about the consequences of sacking this man. He sat at dawn on the wooden stairs at the back of the house, looking over the rice fields. His mind was captured and courage was infused by one thought (either his own, or gleaned from Charles Williams's or C. S. Lewis's writings), "Next Tuesday all the powers of *heaven* are going to be let loose when the man is sacked."

'Now it is Tuesday and all has gone as planned. The man has been sacked. We had promised to tell no one for three days to give him the opportunity to leave secretly to avoid losing face. Only five missionaries know. It has been lonely carrying this for months without the moral and prayer support of others. Thais tend to share things freely, so we presume that it is only a matter of hours and everyone will know what has happened.

'What are my reactions, now it is over?

'First of all I am *scared*. I was drifting to sleep after lunch. Suddenly the doorbell clanged throughout this barn of a house. I was terrified in case it was the man or one of his friends with a gun. It was not. (I should have known better.)

'I am *ashamed*. I am embarrassed to walk past his house. When I met his lovable daughter in the drive this afternoon my smile froze on my face. I had to look the child straight in the eye and remind myself that his sacking was just. He had been repeatedly warned. He knew what would happen if things did not change.

'I also feel *guilty*. Why did we allow our fellow Christian brother to be exposed to temptation too great to resist? Why had it been so easy for him to do wrong? How much were we to blame?

'I feel deep *sympathy*. Where would he go? How would he

earn a living? What about his children's schooling? Apparently his wife only learnt today of what had been going on. How will this affect their marriage?

'We have genuinely loved this man. Somehow he and his family are part of us. *His pain hurts us more deeply because it is we who have had to inflict it.* We can never be the same again. We do not know his heart or his reactions, for being Thai he will have feelings that differ from ours. We know he is hurt. We long to comfort but cannot, nor is there any opiate we can render ...

'I went for coffee with my neighbour, but was 'phoned and asked to return quickly. On the doorstep the man's wife was weeping her goodbyes. She was *thanking* me for all the love and care she had received from me(*me*? when? what?). I put my arms around her and wept with her. She told me that she and the children would live in one room in the market while her husband went out to try and earn a living in the fields. He had been toppled off his pedestal and his life was shattered. The family had to stay in the market here as the school nearest their fields is of poor standard. Anyway they do not even possess a hut (only a shelter) where their fields are. I had to lead this woman who was weeping publicly with shame and grief to a car where a crowd of Thais wept openly around the man. He huddled in the corner of the back seat. He seemed to have shrunk. His eyes did not leave the floor of the car. I gave the customary Thai greeting and raised the palms of my hands together to denote respect for him. For many years we had greeted one another in this way. The car moved away at funeral pace.

'I cannot share my feelings with my friends for this matter must remain confidential until it reaches me from an outside source.

'I went shopping and called into the medicine shop run by a Thai ex-member of the hospital staff. She, a Thai, was someone with whom I could talk. We had been on duty together one morning when I heard by post that one of my children had broken an arm far away at boarding school. This Thai nurse had just heard that her baby had irreversible brain damage. We were united as mothers. Differences in race, language, and religion were irrelevant. In the seclusion of the hospital injection room we knew the mutual comfort of being able to weep for and with one another. We had worked together for years until she left the hospital to care for her mentally retarded child full-time and to run her own business. I was drawn to this Thai friend. I visited her infrequently but she was someone who had known me for a long time. She could see beneath my forced smile and pretty clothes and sense my need of help.

'Her words came straight to the point, "I've worked with you and Dr John for so many years that I know all this has hurt you." In the Thai language she chose words that were gentle and soothing.

'She was one of the few whom I could ask a question only a Thai person could answer, "Can I go and visit the man and his wife? I'm worried about them. How will they live?"

'Had she replied, "Of course not. Your husband sacked him." I would not have been surprised.

'Her smile gave me courage, "Go, you'll be all right. He knows you as well as I do . . ."

'I went to the room that was now his only home. I sat with the curious who had come to observe the man who was the centre of current gossip. I hoped to indicate by this simple action that I still loved him as a person and had not cut him off. There was little else I could do to try to communicate this to him.'

To have to act justly, and hurt people who are loved is a painful business. Sometimes it is more painful to be on the giving end than the receiving end. Sometimes we need to remind ourselves that this may be more hurtful to God than to us humans.

CHAPTER FOUR

Identification means suffering

DAILY experiences in unusual situations have made this truth more real to me than it has been before.

My diary records, 'I had been "on call" for emergencies since 7 a.m. and was due to go "off duty" at 7 p.m. Just before 7 p.m. a police car with flashing lights pulled up in the darkness outside the accident unit of the hospital. All the hospital beds were full. The anaesthetist was off sick and could not work. I routinely requested that the police should take the patient to the Government hospital a few miles away.

'I reached automatically for the patient's pulse to check that he was able to travel. His skin was cold and clammy. He was conscious and moaning. Theoretically we could not receive the man, but looking at his battered body I knew that love forbade sending him away. We dispensed with all routine hospital formalities. I injected morphine intravenously, set up a transfusion, ordered blood, and held an oxygen mask over his face. I could see that all action must be quick or the man would be dead within minutes.

'When I had completed all urgent procedures I examined him thoroughly. The truth was obvious. He was too severely injured to live. I ran my hand up and down his rib cage. The bones were so smashed that I felt as if my fingers were gliding over multiple small pebbles. Such injury must have damaged his lungs, possibly his heart, and probably ruptured his spleen.

'He became quieter and paler. His heart stopped. While I held his hand his reflex gasping ceased. My role, in the end, had been to administer the medical final rites, and to try to make death less frightening for an injured man. He was a stranger of a different nationality from me.

'He died when it was time for me to come "off duty".

'I was now relieved from the discipline of holding back my emotions so that they did not interfere with my performance as a doctor. I was free to allow them to re-assert themselves. This death occurred on the final night of a conference of 200 OMF missionaries taking place at Manorom hospital. Once "off duty" I joined them in the final communion service.

'I felt more human and vulnerable than I had for a long time. A man had been so battered that he had died as I attempted to save him. I could not forget him.

'I wished to be left alone in silence, and resented the hymn singing around me. I could think of nothing but the sacramental significance of the communion service. I had just witnessed a man die in circumstances that reminded me of Jesus' death. "My" man was alone, his father was not with him. None of us knew who he was. The police saw that he died in an orderly fashion, and was given medical help.

'Unexpectedly I remembered a wound penetrating into one side of his abdomen. Jesus' death became very real at that moment. Blood and a watery exudate had seeped out, "God," I wanted to cry, "Jesus was pierced like that wasn't he?"

'The reality of Jesus' death was overwhelming. I forgot I was surrounded by fellow missionaries. I suppose this will be the only time that I shall go from the death of one who died in a manner reminiscent to that of Jesus, straight to a communion service. I could begin to identify with the man, Jesus, who had been crucified.

'The death of Jesus Christ can never be just a beautiful picture, a crucifix, a stained glass window, or something sung about in pious phrases like, "Thy blessed death upon the precious cross". It had been a real and terrible death.'

Someone who read those words commented, 'I cannot free my mind (nor do I wish to) from the broken body of the casualty in your hospital and its terrible affinity with the broken body of the Lord's Supper. Some day you should read Bernard Walke's *Twenty years at St Hilary*. (St Hilary is a haunted and holy Cornish parish where the eccentric and saintly Father Walke worked.) Father Walke set a crucifix at the end of the bed of one of his parishioners, a farm labourer dying in great pain. "I would at times be overcome with the sense of the terrible intimacy that existed between the figure on the Cross and the body distorted in pain lying on the bed – an intimacy which reduced to nothingness all our human activity. Pointing to the crucifix he said to me, 'I feel him working powerfully in me. He must have his way before his work is done.' " "

I am deeply aware that in identification with our human suffering, and especially by his death on the cross, that God is inexplicably bound up with the suffering of the world he created. He knows, cares, and, even more inexplicable, he suffers beyond human comprehension in our human suffering. The total mystery is beyond our intellectual understanding. It is one of those deep mysteries that I *know* to be true. The small measure of suffering that has been entrusted to me has taught me more deeply that God who is love, is good. He is all powerful and understands and is involved in all our human pain. This is part of the mystery of the cross and that which Jesus accomplished there.

Because God is involved, I cannot disengage myself from the world's suffering. If it is all of deep, deep significance to him, then can I pretend that the horror facing much of the world is not happening? Certainly not. I cannot pretend that others in different continents who have different needs from mine, are nothing to do with me, for I know that each human being is of deep significance to God.

If God's love extends to the hurt and suffering of the entire world then dare I close my heart? As far as I am able to understand what is going on I must respond at the deepest levels of myself. I must be concerned and, when appropriate, act where I encounter areas of human need.

March 30th, 1975 was one of those days when I could not escape the suffering occurring in the countries surrounding my home in Thailand.

The weather was hot, temperatures running between 90° and 100°F. with high humidity due to flooded rice fields around the house.

I wrote, 'One day it will be good to go to England again and to be able to get *into* bed. Meanwhile I have been so tired that I spent most of the day *on* my bed. It is too hot to be covered by even a sheet. Now I feel invigorated and ready for the crowds who will be waiting to be treated in hospital tomorrow. Over this Easter weekend, for the first time ever, the hospital has been closed for all but emergency cases. We all need the break.

'In a corner of our living room we have displayed the latest two covers of *Time Magazine*. They clearly signify what is happening around Thailand. Last week the caption on the cover read, THE GROWING TRAGEDY. The cover picture was a beautiful Cambodian mother with her teenage daughter. Their dove-like eyes communicated a mixture of peace and hopelessness. Today's cover bears seven letters only: RETREAT. Beneath the word is a bewildered Vietnamese peasant cradling his bleeding, dying son. I have just enough faith left in God in the face of recent events to tie a scarlet thread from these two magazine covers to link them to a poster proclaiming JESUS IS ALIVE TODAY and the three letters BUT which join these three sheets of paper together. Cambodia and Vietnam at the moment are cover story facts of the mass media news coverage. That Jesus is alive and concerned in what is happening is a fact that faith alone dares to believe.

'*The Bangkok Post* newspaper for Easter Sunday carried a story that shocked me deeply. After reading it I could not go to church and sing in the joy of the resurrection. I could not sing. The thought of people in the West eating chocolate Easter eggs, parading new Easter bonnets, and rejoicing in churches full of spring flowers, contrasted sharply with the desolation of those whose story I was reading. I spent that Easter day alone trying to come to terms with the faith that assured me that the resurrection was a fact when the news media appeared to proclaim the opposite.'

In retrospect I am surprised by how much events in countries around Thailand affected me. I don't understand why I should have cared so much.

I ate little and wept much that Easter Sunday. God showed me that he loved South East Asia. I sensed that I was being allowed to experience something for which I had often prayed, 'I want to know Christ and the power of his resurrection and the fellowship of sharing in his sufferings, becoming like him in his death' (Philippians 3.10).

God was suffering over the events of that day and allowed me mystical insight into his concern.

On Easter day, March 30th 1975, *The Bangkok Post* carried the story I shall never forget about Vietnam as it was collapsing.

'Only the fastest, the strongest, and the meanest of the huge mob got a ride in the last plane from Da Nang yesterday. People died trying to get aboard and others died as they fell thousands of feet into the sea because even desperation could no longer keep their fingers welded to the undercarriage.

'It was a flight into hell and only a good American pilot and a lot of prayer got us back . . . alive . . . More than a thousand people had been waiting around Quonset, several hundred yards from where we touched down.

'Suddenly it was a mob in motion . . . they whirred across the tarmac . . . speeded by sheer desperation and panic.

' . . . there wasn't room for everybody, and everybody knew damn well that there wasn't.

'Daley (the pilot) and I were knocked aside and backward. If Daley thought he'd get some women and children out of Da Nang, he was wrong. The plane was jammed in an instant with soldiers, troops of the 1st division's meanest unit, the Black Panthers.

'They literally ripped the clothes off Daley, along with some of his skin. I saw some of them kick an old woman in the face to get aboard. In the movies, somebody would have shot the bastard and helped the old lady onto the plane. This was no movie. The bastard flew and the old lady was tumbling down the tarmac, her fingers clawing towards the plane that was already rolling.

'A back-up 727 had flown behind us but had been ordered not to land when the panic broke out. He radioed that he could see the legs of people hanging down from the under-carriage of the plane.

' . . . saw at least one person lose his grip on life and plummet into the South China sea below.

' . . . There were 288 or more people jammed into the cabin of the little 727 limping down the coast. Only two women and one baby among them. The rest were soldiers . . .

'The last plane from Da Nang was one hell of a ride . . . but the face that remains is that of the old woman lying flat on the tarmac seeing hope, seeing life itself just off the ends of her fingertips and rolling the other way.'

That Easter Day I glimpsed what it means to begin to be identified with Jesus when he suffered a cruel human death, and the mental and physical agony preceding it. I gained insight into the Apostle Paul's words for the Colossian Christians, 'Now I rejoice in what was suffered for you, and I fill up in my flesh what is still lacking in regard to Christ's afflictions, for the sake of his body which is the church. I have become its servant by the commission God gave me to present to you the word of God in its fullness – the mystery that has been kept hidden for ages and generations, but is now disclosed to the saints. To them God has chosen to make known among the Gentiles the glorious riches of this mystery, which is Christ in you, the hope of glory' (Colossians 1:24–27).

On Easter Day, 1979 some friends wrote me a letter I found strangely comforting. Their only baby had been still-born a few years ago, 'Hannah's grave when visited on Easter Day thrilled us by being covered with primroses and violets planted last year and all flourishing – it actually looked *beautiful*. And we could only stop and wonder at such newness: risen indeed!'

My inexplicable emotional suffering had some purpose I do not fully understand. It seemed to be part of God's longing to reveal himself in an uncaring world which had ignored or rejected him for centuries.

Throughout 1975 I lived in Thailand. Yet I wept and prayed for Cambodia, Vietnam, and Laos as these lands faced convulsions that led them to Communist domination. The newspaper continually kept the hard truths before me.

On 9th May 1975, after Phnom Penh had fallen, I read about the city in *The Bangkok Post*, 'Two million people in stunned silence: walking, cycling, pushing cars, covering the roads like a human carpet: suddenly forced to abandon the capital.'

I knew of many who had recently become Christians in Cambodia. Young, old, educated, illiterate, fit, and amputees in hospital had been turning to Christ in thousands. My reactions made the Bible words real, 'If one part suffers, every part suffers with it' (1 Corinthians 12:36). I did not know these people. Why did I care? God knows.

The cold newspaper print spoke about my brothers in Christ, 'Hospitals jammed with the wounded, being emptied down to the last patient. These people too ... limping, crawling, on crutches, carried on someone's back, lying on beds being wheeled up a road: ordered out of the city.

'And Phnom Penh itself. Once throbbing, now an echo chamber of silent streets lined with abandoned cars and gaping, empty shops, while the street lights burned early for a population no longer there ...'

I glimpsed the nightmare that was reality. A nightmare

which in 1979 became blacker as further war fell on that land.

Many of us need the courage to try to understand what we read in the newspapers or watch on television news programmes. Something that happened far away may be transformed so that it seems too near for comfort. Home truths hurt. Yet I believe this is the kind of hurting, or cross bearing, in which Christians must participate as they share Christ's sufferings for his world.

I find little excuse for the popular Christian magazine which in October 1979 stated, 'News of life in Cambodia is only just seeping out to the West after four-and-a-half years of silence. In an exclusive report . . . ' The news had been available for five years but most of the world refused to listen to it.

George MacDonald's writings sustained me in days which could have sometimes been mistaken for nights in 1975. On 9th May, having read of the evacuation of Phnom Penh, I read words of hope from *Lilith*, 'Hark to the golden cock! Far away – and in the heart of the Aenian silence I heard a jubilant cry of the golden throat. It hurled defiance at death and the dark; sang of infinite hope and coming calms. It was the expectation of the creature finding at last a voice; a cry over chaos that would be a kingdom.'[2]

This was all tied up with the incredible hope contained in the New Testament, 'I consider that our present sufferings are not worth comparing with the glory that will be revealed in us. The creation waits in eager expectation for the sons of God to be revealed. For the creation was subjected to frustration, not by its own choice, but by the will of the one who subjected it, in hope that the creation itself will be liberated from its bondage to decay and brought into the glorious freedom of the children of God.

'We know that the whole creation has been groaning as in the pains of childbirth right up to the present time. Not only so, but we ourselves, who have the first fruits of the Spirit, groan inwardly as we await eagerly for our adoption as sons, the redemption of our bodies' (Romans 8:18–23).

Through all this I cling to the fact that God suffered as man, and that he suffers now with his world. As I am united to him, so I too am permitted to be involved in a mysterious and inexplicable measure in human suffering in countries I have never visited. Through Jesus and my identification with him I am part of this.

God suffers with those who suffer. I cannot explain how this can be. I am invited simply to share with him in his suffering if I wish to achieve that for which I was created: if I desire to be more like Jesus Christ.

[1] *Twenty Years at St Hilary,*   Bernard Walke.
[2] *Lilith,*   George MacDonald.

CHAPTER FIVE

Hope when helpless

Many of the medical staff and patients on his ward in a famous London teaching hospital watched him with amazement.

There was an indefinable quality about this man that went beyond the ordinary. He knew he had cancer and under two years left in which to live. He was aware that medically the outlook was hopeless. He had been informed that nothing further could be done to help him. Medical students studied him as an interesting 'case history'. However their interest went beyond him as a patient for they found that his personality was infinitely more gripping than his rare illness.

This man, living under sentence of death, was one to whom those who were healthy were drawn to obtain encouragement. They could see that his faith, hope and love were infectious.

Christian medical students visited him regularly for advice and support as they sought to make their Christianity real in an environment that rejected Christian values. His unquenchable faith gave them courage. His practical love to other patients fitter than he was made people question, 'Why are you different?'

He was joyful and convincing as he replied, 'In death I have nothing to lose but this world. I've everything to gain in the immense treasure I believe waits for me in the new life after life on earth.'

His life was the means through which several other patients entered into a similar experience of Christ. They too began to know God as one who gives hope in seemingly hopeless situations.

This patient's special love for medical students who were known to be Christians made them feel that in him they had an elder brother to whom they could turn when they were in trouble. Two years later he was readmitted to hospital to die and this love was practically reciprocated.

One of those medical students, my husband, John, was by then a new doctor. He recalls the emaciated form of this patient who had so encouraged him as a young student, now lying helpless in bed. A thin arm with tendons and bones clearly outlined, beckoned him over to the bedside.

John was used to encouragement from this man. He now heard a dying patient whisper to him, 'Please pray with me. I'm too weak to pray any more.'

He looked into the eyes of his dying friend and saw the light of hope still flickering in one on whom he had once leaned for support. Now this man needed his help. He prayed as requested, marvelling that despite suffering this man *still* trusted in God. He never lost his assurance that God was all powerful and could have healed him if he wanted to. He recognised that God had not chosen to cure him, and accepted it quietly.

For many years after this patient's death his memory has brought alive one of the central challenges of Christianity to my husband. This man hoped with inextinguishable faith despite the seeming hopelessness of his illness. The spring of his hope was his God.

Faith, hope and love are not separated in the New Testament. They were demonstrated in their unity in the life of this patient. Frequently the writers of the letters in the New Testament link these three ingredients of Christianity together, and it is helpful to think of them as a whole unit, as well as in separate parts. 'And now these three remain: faith, *hope* and love. But the greatest of these is love' (1 Corinthians 13:13).

The link is explained a little by the words, 'Love always protects, always trusts, always hopes, always perseveres. Love never fails . . . ' (1 Corinthians 13:7, 8).

The intermingling of these three is taken for granted in words like, 'we have heard of your faith in Christ Jesus and of the love you have for all the saints – the faith and love that spring from the hope that is stored up for you in heaven, and that you have already heard about in the word of truth, the gospel that has come to you' (Colossians 1:4, 5).

This leads us to ask the question, 'What is our hope as Christians?'

'Come to Jesus. Accept him tonight as your Saviour, and

your life will be filled with joy from now onwards.' How often we have heard such words from platforms.

Yet these words speak only half truths. A Christian encounters not only a pure, deep, God-given joy but he also meets the intertwined threads of suffering which are joy's partners in human life. The man who has the capacity to rejoice deeply is one who often suffers much.

It would be more realistic for a preacher to proclaim, 'Come to Jesus and you will find a rich, fulfilling joy. You will also enter into a new understanding of suffering. God will impart joy that can only be a foretaste of heaven. Then, as you face suffering you will discover untapped resources of strength to see you through.'

Christianity is not some kind of innoculation to give immunity from suffering. Slushy religious songs which proclaim this to be so delude us, so that we are baffled when suffering strikes us, and want to abandon even the little faith we have embraced. We may feel we have been duped.

If Christianity proved to be a talisman against this world's sufferings then how easily we would misuse it! Some of us would see it as a key by which we could wind up the almighty God like a clockwork toy to make him work on our behalf. When a problem arose, we would only have to turn the key and he would automatically act as we wanted him to.

Perhaps such an extreme shows us how wrong a direction some of us unconsciously pursue. We begin to think, 'I am a Christian and so my loving Father will not let me suffer.' And we end up by concluding, 'I am a Christian and therefore must be immune from suffering.' Life and the teaching of the Bible prove this is wrong.

God promises us, 'No temptation has seized you except what is common to man. And God is faithful; he will not let you be tempted beyond what you can bear. But when you are tempted, he will also provide a way out so that you can stand up under it' (1 Corinthians 10:13).

All this says something loud and clear which I need to hear and hold in my heart. It proclaims that God still is in this universe and that when he permits us to go through suffering, then he knows exactly what is happening to us and precisely how much we can bear as individuals. Perhaps the suffering we endure may overwhelm us and so in total love God relieves us completely by taking us from this world to the new home we enter through death. I believe in a God who has set up a world which runs according to the laws he has set. God has given man both the free will and the power to rule the world as man decides. Sadly, man's methods and God's often differ. The world is no longer the place it was intended to be. Suffering has entered our world as a result.

God has the power to cause suffering to cease immediately, but the nature of the world he has set up is such that this power is rarely exercised. I know that God is strong enough to stop bad things from happening. Yet having given man freedom to exercise his free will, God rarely intervenes to stop evil. Rather, God imparts courage and strength to see us through suffering. Suffering is not wasted, for God often uses it to help us grasp his truth more deeply and to become more mature as Christians.

For years I have wondered, 'God, why have you allowed me to go through peculiar experiences in the past few years. Why so much bereavement, and why this inexplicable concern for Cambodia?' Only now, in December 1979, do I begin to glimpse that God had to change me, so that I could do a job he had for me. I would have gone to pieces unless God had taught me lessons I needed to know before I visited refugee camps in Thailand and Hong Kong in November 1979.

This is what I wrote in the middle of an emotionally and physically exhausting tour of human tragedy in November 1979, 'The rosy cheeked English children hide their sweets under their sweaters from the penetrating stare of their Sunday school teacher. Most would prefer to be at home in front of the TV. Sunday lunch has filled them and they are drowsy. They sing as instructed, "I know a fount where sins are washed away," the teacher interrupts them to try to get two boys in the back row to pay more attention to the words and less to something they are hiding from her. Most thoughts are elsewhere on more relevant themes, like James Bond, the pop charts; very definitely miles away from the words of the hymn.

'They press on reluctantly, "I know a place where night is turned to day, burdens are lifted . . . " and so they go on.

'While they sing on that Sunday in November 1979, I slump disheartened, thirsty, and more tired than I can ever remember in a place called Sakeo (translated it means "Crystal Pool") in a refugee camp in East Thailand near the

Cambodian borders. I am 9,000 miles away in space from those children in England.

'We have seen the plight of the Cambodian refugees on TV. For us the magnitude of the problem can be locked up in a box when we switch it off, have had enough, and want to banish thought. "Out of sight, out of mind" is all too true for us.

'In that refugee camp, Sakeo, the horror of the situation cannot be turned off when we have had enough.

'30,000 Cambodians, squatting in the jungle on the Thai side of the Cambodian border, had been piled into buses and shipped to Sakeo out of range of Vietnamese cross-border fire, three weeks before I arrived. The politics behind this is there for you to read in your newspaper.

'On this November day I have no time to think of politics, for people consume everything I can offer. They are sick and I am a doctor. I can work to help them and work I have. These people in "Crystal Pool" know nothing of cleansing fountains where the filth of days of jungle living and the sweat of fear and flight covering their bodies could be washed away. Some have begun to find strength to make it to the water cisterns. Others, still too exhausted, lie on mats on the earth floor. Of fountains that cleanse hearts they know nothing. Many of these people were Khmer Rouge soldiers, their dependants, or civilians forced to stay with the soldiers.

'They squat in their thousands on scrubland quickly and efficiently cleared for them. Each remnant of a family (I have seen few complete families: all here are bereaved) has laid a mat on the ground on a piece of earth the size of a hearth rug. They stick a few bamboo sticks into the ground, and drape something like a blue, a green or grey sheet of plastic table cloth in tent-like fashion to make a tiny home. Our current fussing about mortgages and soaring costs of houses seems preposterous in the face of these people in such a situation. The 30,000 live with barely room to walk between their dwellings. Over-crowding is such that the onset of an epidemic would spell the potential decimation of this fragment of Cambodia's exodus. Many of the very sick are unable to make their way through the crowds to the hospital areas.

'The heat consumes us as we pick our way through something like a colony of human birds' nests. The people wear black – the traditional worldwide colour for mourning – the colour which the Khmer Rouge had deemed fitting to be worn by everyone in Cambodia during their brutal regime. As I look at them I see symbolically a doomed race wearing its mourners' shrouds while still alive in a kind of death. Over the 30,000 hovers a frightening silence. People are quiet. They barely move but sit placidly baking in the sun under their sheets of plastic roofs. I touch the bodies of those lying motionless. Many are dehydrated, many burn with fever, many cough with acute pneumonia or chronic TB. Some lie unconscious from cerebral malaria or meningitis.

'The children are listless and malnourished. Fifteen-year-olds look the size of ten-year-olds but have faces like Methuselah. Babies hardly cry, and barely have the strength to suck milk. Most mothers have no supply of breast milk for their babies so severe malnutrition is not uncommon. Little children do not cry. They hardly move, and they certainly do not play.

'Mirrored in the horror of this tragedy at "Crystal Pool" I vaguely see a reflection. I cannot see my own face clearly (just as well, as the dust, dirt, and exhaustion of two days' working here do not make me very glamorous). In the reflection I can clearly see a familiar figure as he comes behind me, lays his gentle hands on my shoulders and whispers, "As my Father has sent me, even so send I you." At his bidding I pick myself up, and continue working as a doctor. I came to find facts and to collect statistics but this acute need demands my medical expertise.

'The One who commissions me is no stranger to human tragedy. Six weeks earlier I had opened my heart to Mother Theresa in Calcutta, as we talked together as two women. I had shared the wound there has been in my heart for the past four years as I had known what was happening to the Cambodians under the Khmer Rouge regime. Her steady gaze, and strong voice spoke words to the effect that Cambodia was the "open Calvary of our age". I never doubted her; I agreed with what she was saying. At that time I had not anticipated standing at the foot of this Calvary myself so soon, and trying to be one of those who would not quietly acquiesce to another crucifixion.

'Bodies are piling up in a nearby tent which serves as a mortuary (hundreds of thousands have already died in Cambodia). The local Buddhist cemetery can no longer cope with so many daily cremations and a Chinese firm has accepted the contract for emptying the mortuary tent daily. Bodies are piled up like sacks of flour in that tent. A human life hardly seems of significance. There are already too many who are alive who cannot be catered for with the dignity that a human life deserves (and thousands more are coming from the Thai/Cambodia border). Does it matter if they leave this life daily in their twenties and relieve a little of the back-breaking burden from those who can barely cope?

'But in the hospital section of the camp I have seen that people and individuals matter very much. The world has responded to Sakeo's agonised cry for help. There are many people of different races and creeds who care for the sick and the dying, and for the orphans. The hospital started in tents, then was improved to shacks, and is now wards of large thatch-roofed, mat-walled, gravel-floored buildings. Not all the wards have beds, and the sick lie on mats on the earth floor. Two weeks before in a monsoon rain storm, thirty patients drowned in one night when the plastic roof of their shelter was whipped away by the gale. They were discovered dead in the light of day.

'Medical teams slog from dawn to dusk. No one thinks of lunch breaks . . . as for coffee or tea breaks these are merely happy thoughts since one is lucky to find a glass of water in this barren spot in the middle of nowhere. Under such work pressures an occasional day off becomes a medical worker's sole hope of survival. For some non-Christians sleep is only possible at night with the help of drugs and drink to blot out the daytime nightmare from night's dark hours.

'Christians are among the many relief workers who have responded to the need of Sakeo. I met people from Tear Fund Holland, Tear Fund New Zealand, Tear Fund UK, World Vision Thailand, World Vision International, American Baptists, the American Christian and Missionary Alliance working with the World Relief Commission, as well as teams of Roman Catholics. In the International Red Cross team of eight, who search the camp of 30,000 to carry in those who are too ill to get themselves to the hospital, I met a fine Christian nurse from Scotland.

'God cares about this human tragedy. His children are there along with the others who have responded to this acute need. No one is standing on one side acquiescing to the crucifixion of Cambodia. Among foreigners who speak Cambodian I met Mr Norman Ens, a Church and Missionary Alliance missionary, and Don Cormack, an OMF missionary. Both have formerly worked in Phnom Penh. They seem to do anything and everything. They carry the sick from the camp to the hospital, they translate for doctors, they comfort the bereaved, act as social workers and move in and out of the pitiful shelters of the refugees telling of a Creator God who is love. What is love to a people who have been taught to hate? Perhaps they begin to see it in the faces of those who care for the sick. No longer are the sick a useless encumbrance to be shot or left behind in the jungle. In the hospital units of Sakeo they are loved, washed, fed, and given medical help.

'Due to the witness of lives and the voices of Cambodian speaking missionaries, by mid-November 1979 eight Khmers had found the ultimate reality and salvation that is in Jesus Christ.

'Even if it were possible to transform Sakeo into a crystal-clear, healing stream overnight – a stream in which the sick were healed, families united, people fed and clothed, and emotional wounds healed, I still do not believe this would be the total answer. I see the only real answer in the God of Christianity. The deepest needs of those who have committed or who have been subjected to the Khmer Rouge atrocities can be dealt with only in the immense forgiveness flowing from Calvary. The dehumanisation of a race can be righted when one man recognises and is able to love another he formerly hated because he has become his brother in Christ. The hopelessness of the future can be transformed into the supreme hope that is promised to those whose lives are bound up in the present and future hope which exists in Jesus Christ alone.

'So let the children of the West go on singing their song about fountains where sins are washed away, and night is turned to day. Children must sing this song throughout the centuries. The ethos of their song must reach those other children who are living in a kind of death in the heartland and all around the borders of Cambodia. Their song is the only source of ultimate hope. May it reach those children I saw in Sakeo, who huddle apathetically, silently stretching stick-like limbs over swollen bellies. They are the future of the Cambodian race.

'The veteran, hardened journalists tell me that this is "worse than Bangladesh". I do not disagree with them.'

I am grateful to God for the lessons he has taught me in the past few years which enabled me to cope emotionally with the immense human suffering in which I was involved in Sakeo. I am grateful, too, to find that my eternal hope in God is deepened by the experiences through which I have passed.

Incidents recorded in the Bible indicate that God has on special occasions put an end to suffering and that he has not abdicated his power to intervene when he sees it is right to do so. Intervention is the exception rather than the rule. Our God is not only all powerful but he is also good and loving. This is all connected to the hope which we are given as Christians that life involves more than the things we are able to see. We are bound by time but our faith exists in eternity and is not limited by our human concepts of the temporal.

Again we must ask the question, 'What is our hope as Christians?'

I believe that the New Testament leads us to understand that it is something that we as Christians must actively set ourselves to pursue. Hope is a gift God offers us which we must set our wills to grasp. In a world of hopelessness, meaninglessness, and lack of direction we have decided to follow Christ. In doing this we face the challenge and the possibility that we can be people whose lives are characterised by a shining hope. A hope that relates both to the present and to a future after this life is over.

'Surely I haven't suffered that I, my crimes and my sufferings, may manure the soil of the future harmony for someone else. I want to see with my own eyes the hind lie down with the lion and the victim rise up and embrace his murderer. I want to be there when everyone understands what it has all been for.' Dostoevsky's desire will probably be denied us. We need to be able to accept that this will be a fact in our lives.

I find, in the works of Albert Camus, the humanist, words directed at me, 'The world expects of Christians that they will raise their voices so loudly and clearly and so formulate their protests that not even the simplest man can have the slightest doubt about what they are saying . . . we stand in need of folk who have determined to speak directly and unmistakably and, come what may, to stand by what they have said.'

We are challenged when life is hard to exercise the hope that is potentially ours if we are Christians. We are challenged to show the hope that is part of Christianity.

We can find comfort as we face life's troubles, 'May our Lord Jesus Christ himself and God our Father, who loved us and by his grace gave us eternal encouragement and good hope, encourage your hearts and strengthen you in every good deed and word' (2 Thessalonians 2:16).

This attitude is required when life is tough, 'Therefore prepare your minds for action; be self-controlled; set your hope fully on the grace to be given you when Jesus Christ is revealed' (1 Peter 1:13).

These words are familiar. It is therefore important that we reassess their meaning in our own lives.

There is an element in Christian hope which makes us grit our teeth and refuse to deny our faith however bad things get, 'Let us hold unswervingly to the hope we profess, for he who promised is faithful' (Hebrews 10:23).

We must turn from depression and hopelessness, and deliberately look at the God of hope.

Such hope is something which can impart extraordinary joy to the mundane lives of most of us who are ordinary Christians.

We are *commanded* 'Be joyful in your hope' (Romans 12:12).

Our problem is that we either take this hope for granted, or we have failed to realise what it is all about, and so we live lives similar to everyone else, and lose the joy that is potentially ours.

Such hope enables Christians to continue in seemingly hopeless situations. I marvel at stories of Cambodian Christians who have crossed over into Thailand.

I am tempted to speculate, 'If I were one of them would I have the courage to act as they did?'

Such speculation is a waste of time, for until our faith is put under pressure we cannot know how we will react.

Stories of Cambodian refugee Christians convinced me that their hope in God has not been futile. We know that many have died, and many are dying, and many will die, still grasping their eternal hope. Others, however, have lived to share their stories of the way in which God helped them in their extremity.

One young woman, a new Christian, longed to escape to a land where she would be free to worship the Christian God. She fled with relatives, hiding in jungles and travelling by night to the Thai border. Food was limited, and had to be supplemented by digging up edible jungle roots to eat with a daily handful of boiled rice. When, after many difficulties, the small party reached the borders of Thailand they were nearly starving. The young woman was confident that God was with her, and whether she lived or died she need not abandon herself to the terror of despair. Her hope contrasted sharply with the desperate escape efforts some refugees were making, for they had no Christian faith like hers. Their hope lay only in the hope of freedom.

When she reached the Thai border the situation seemed totally hopeless. The small party encountered a border of land a few hundred yards wide scattered with buried mines that lay between them and freedom. She and the others could see Thailand, but they knew it was now beyond their reach. To turn back meant probable death, but to step forward could mean death, too, if one of their party accidentally trod on a buried land mine.

A young Christian Cambodian man stepped forward, 'I'll go first,' he offered. 'I have no fear of death, and if I tread on a land mine I'll go to be with the Lord. If I get through safely then the rest of you can follow and know that the track I have taken is safe for you, too.'

The others had no time to thank him. He set off quickly and reached Thailand safely in a few minutes. The rest were able to follow his footsteps to freedom.

The young woman was soon secure in a refugee camp. Had she been killed she would have tested the reality of the eternal hope in which her faith rested; that there was life after death. Reaching a refugee camp was not the end of her helplessness. Where could she go from there? Would any country ever receive her now that she was stateless and had left her own land? She waited for a third country to take her, assured that ultimately her destiny lay in a fourth country; heaven. She knew that God was controlling her life, but she knew also that this did not guarantee immunity from the inhumanity man inflicts on man. She suffered months of uncertainty about the future, living in poverty in a refugee camp, trusting that the Bible was true, 'And we know that in all things God works for the good of those who love him' (Romans 8:28).

She knew that if no country would receive her then God would continue to care for her. It was with joy that she learned that a place had been found for her in America with a number of other refugees. Few of the others were Christians, and so she did not feel she was receiving preferential treatment from the Almighty, but rather that this was all part of his plan for her. Wherever men sent her she was able to believe that God was overruling all these events in her life. She is now training to be a doctor.

A vital part of the Christian's hope is his beliefs about life after death; 'If only for this life we have hope in Christ, we are to be pitied more than all men: But Christ has indeed been raised from the dead, the first fruits of those who have fallen asleep' (1 Corinthians 15:19, 20).

'He who did not spare his only son, but gave him up for us all – how will he not also, along with him, graciously give us all things?' (Romans 8:32).

For mortals to speak of heavenly hope goes beyond normal human language. These are concepts that are beyond the grasp of our finite minds. Picture language aids us. Great Christian writers help us glimpse the hope that is ours for the future.

C. S. Lewis speaks of George MacDonald as one to whom he owes a debt for his writings, 'almost as great as one man could owe another'. George MacDonald has left a treasury of books which shine with rays of the glimpses of the glory of the hope that is ours.

He ends one of his novels with the words, 'Something more than the sun, greater than the light is coming, is coming – nonetheless surely coming that it is long upon the road'.[1]

George MacDonald's personal life was full of tragedy. He was severely ill with tuberculosis and nearly died of lung haemorrhages several times. His life story is that of a man who repeatedly faced bereavement. As he viewed his own life and human suffering, it was with the eyes of hope that enabled him to write, 'The end of the Maker's dream is not thus'.

In our hopelessness we are offered the supreme gift of hope.

[1] *Lilith,* George MacDonald.

CHAPTER SIX

To lose a child

A YEAR and a half ago the Christmas roses were flowering in profusion around my former home at Manorom in Thailand. Their scarlet beauty hung high above the lawns like unspilled pools of blood. Twelve lives had been lost in a road accident, and seven children no longer lay the Christmas roses in wreaths round the decorative candles on dining room tables. The silence shrouded the houses and gardens.

My husband, John, flew to Thailand from England to see if he could bring some kind of comfort to the bereaved. He arrived at Manorom, the car door swung open and he fell into the arms of those who had lost some they loved. One face above all shines in his memory. A Swiss missionary mother had lost her youngest son. Her brown hair framed a pale face ravaged by grief. He was at a loss. What could he possibly say to comfort such a one as she? His words would be empty phrases and tired clichés. He was silent.

Her voice rang with conviction, 'John, God is good.'

Three words echoed in his mind, haunting him for months, 'God is good . . . God is good . . . '

Such words from such as she can never be erased from his heart. A mother whose youngest son had been killed needlessly was certain that God was good; so certain that this was the first thing she shared as John arrived, travel-stained and jet-lagged from England.

This mother holds the key which can unlock much of our searching and perplexity. She believes that, despite everything appearing to the contrary, God is still good. As we look at children who die we need to see through eyes like hers. We theorise, but she has walked barefoot along this Via Dolorosa. She has emerged believing against all odds that God is good. This can be our experience too.

Grief for the death of children has always been part of me,

extending even to grief for children I have never known. Letters from a friend in Jerusalem brought the beauty of Jewish children home to me, and colour photographs of Jerusalem's children decorated a corner of my study in Thailand, making real the Bible words about the new Jerusalem, 'The city streets will be filled with boys and girls playing there' (Zechariah 8:5).

From Jerusalem in 1976 I received this communication, 'The museum I believe must be visited on any serious pilgrimage to Jerusalem. It is for some the museum, a memorial to the Holocaust, the genocide of the Jews by Nazi Germany. It is, now, one of the tourist sights of Jerusalem, a place you must "do" – but, despite that, its terrible impact is not lost. It succeeds by a subtle blending of the explicit and the muted, in conveying something of the cosmic scale of that vast crime. Many of the pictures one has seen before and the story is in outline not in its anguished detail. But I confess I was more heartbroken by it here than ever before. The museum's final hall contains a series of black pillars inscribed, in gold letters, with the names of the countries from which the Jews were taken to the death camps – and the numbers of those who perished from each land. One particular column does not stand for a country, at least not in a geographical or political sense. It has one word on it – CHILDREN. Beneath it is a case with a glass front and in the case is one little shoe – taken perhaps from a five-year-old child. The words set against the wall as you leave are "Son of man, keep not silent, forget not deeds of tyranny, cry out at the disaster of a people. Recount it unto your children, and they unto theirs from generation unto generation – how the mighty are fallen, the great in spirit and stout of heart, walking to their death in a halo of eternity." '

The writer finishes, 'Well, what is the logic of *this* letter? I begin with the memorial of the Holocaust, enough to make one believe that the world is ruled by some vile Hindu god of destruction. And yet, at the end of the day, I am convinced that it is not so. The unquenchable joy of our little Jewish guide, who knows the dark story better than any Christian, persuades me that there is hope.'

This letter from Jerusalem to Thailand conveyed to me the tragedy that had occurred during my own happy childhood. As I had played away the days other children had suffered and been murdered. The shoe of the unknown five-year-old in the museum lodged in my memory to reappear with piercing poignancy whenever I encountered beauty.

A Thai lotus flower, pink petals cupped and open to greet the dawn was painful to admire. I knew that by midday the flower would have closed beneath the sun's burning beams. Similarly, Jewish children had played in their life's dawn, then perished in premature dusk.

The solace of the music I listened to, to soften the ugliness of parts of life, ceased with the sudden silence at the end of a record or cassette. With similar suddenness, the laughter of Jewish children had been extinguished.

Beauty, joy, pain and loss, were focused in my mind for many weeks on the shoe I had seen in imagination in a letter from Jerusalem.

I ached for a race, and for its children. I had never known them and yet I was unable to dissociate myself from the new knowledge I had gained. To know was to care, and to care was to be hurt personally by what had happened.

To lose children was a part of my life to which I could never be reconciled. Working in up-country Thailand meant that my own children had been separated from me when they were very small in order to be educated elsewhere. I could not teach them myself and there was no alternative if I was to continue in Thailand other than sending them away for schooling.

I believe in families. I do not believe it is normally right for a family unit to be split up. I was hurt as I went against what seemed to be axiomatic for mankind, and allowed my children to go away from me. All normal rules were being broken, and to be the exception that proves the rule was for me to be humanly hurt. Each time my children came home I knew they must leave again, and faced that day with dread. Past platitudes were no comfort. Partings became harder not easier as the years passed.

Jesus had said, ' "I tell you the truth, no one who has left home or brothers or sisters or mother or father or children or fields for me and the gospel will fail to receive a hundred times as much in this present age (homes, brothers, sisters, mothers, children and fields – and with them persecutions)

48

and in the age to come eternal life" ' (Mark 10:29, 30). The emphasis here in the Greek suggests that what is gained will far outweigh what is lost.

As a mother, I have never fully come to terms with my children being away. To see one's children only once a year from the age of eleven upwards hurts beyond description. Intellectually I may comfort myself with the knowledge that they have excellent guardians but as a mother I ache with the pain of premature partings from my children.

Comfort was given through other people's children. One evening I travelled to Bangkok sitting on a mattress at the back of a van cradling a sleeping Swiss infant in my arms. This child satisfied my longing for my own children by his physical presence and tiny heart beating near mine for the hour and a half journey. Little Lucas was a gift to me that night. His presence and proximity provided deep comfort. Another child, a dentist's son, too young yet for school, occasionally plied me with the endless questions I had tried to answer patiently when my own children had been with me. Little Johnny never allowed a visitor to be bored. A minute New Zealand doll-like creature allowed me to give her painful injections when she was ill, and instead of running away from me, would run to greet me with arms outstretched to be cuddled. This doll, aged two, attached herself to my son like a limpet. Wherever he went, Adele went too. Becky, aged four, and their neighbour's British daughter Rachel, aged seven, symbolised to me all that was perfect in childhood. They were beautiful to look at, they were accepting and trustful of me, a mere adult, who from time to time intruded on their world. If they cried or argued or were disobedient – as they must have been for they were not angels – then I can no longer remember it. Rachel worked hard trying to train her younger brother Mark, aged three, not to let down the family; he did his best to please his big, important sister.

These children surrounded me at home alone in Thailand when my own children were away at school, and unknowingly eased my sense of loss. I took them for granted, and forgot to savour the precious moments when I was alone with them. They flew kites, reared hens from eggs hatched under lamps in the bedroom, built dykes, and wove their stories and games around the banana groves and pineapple plants in our joint gardens. They were an exquisite backdrop to the intensely serious adult life I led as a doctor in the hospital. I was foolish to take them for granted.

Then suddenly in a road accident in 1978 each one of these young children was killed.

As I write these words in 1979 in Thailand silence has replaced the sounds of shouting, screaming, laughing and crying in the gardens near my home. No children play here any more.

I was on leave at the time. I looked around my living room in England, and saw walls covered with posters of beautiful children. I found plants that had died while I had been away for two weeks. The room reeked of death; dead plants and dead children. I needed to feel the life which faith assured me was already there in death's new life. So I filled the room with new growing plants and fresh spring-like pictures. The only picture I kept of children was one of two little ones, representative of those killed at Manorom, gazing through a window pane in the rain as if under the shadow of a cross and a sea of tears.

That children should die can never be understood. Only in the cross can I begin to sense that there might be some meaning to an apparently pointless waste of life. I cannot grasp its full significance. Yet I find I must meditate on the cross to make some way of life possible in the face of such seemingly senseless disaster.

A Son hung on a cross and cried in agony to his Father. His Father, God, was inexplicably one with the Son, and suffered with him and in him. God knows what it is like to be human and to be hurt. God suffers when we are hurt. He suffers with each child and adult who suffers. In the mystery of the cross I can derive comfort for these children I have loved who have now left me. I cannot understand. I set my will to trust that God is good, even if the evidence appears to be to the contrary.

God knows how I feel facing the perplexity of human loss. I can state the simple fact that despite my intellect informing me sometimes that it appears that God cannot be good, I *know* this is not true. Within my heart is the knowledge that God is good.

CHAPTER SEVEN

To be human — to be hurt

I HAVE listened to countless sermons. I have heard many pat answers on how to meet grief when it strikes. Few, however, tell me how to handle my grief when it hits personally and unexpectedly. Through my own experience, I believe that a large part of the answer to this lies in the fact that although we are Christians we are still human, and so we meet grief, both as Christians and as ordinary human beings.

My children wept when they heard of Twink's death in the accident at Manorom in 1978.

Later, regaining composure, they compared their last words with her before they left for England, as they sat together at the back of the car. They were reacting normally, not hiding behind a façade that everything was all right, when everything for the time being seemed to be all wrong.

One remembered, 'She promised me a party next time we met in the summer for passing my "O" levels.'

Twink used everything and anything as an excuse for a party, and time to have fun together.

Another added, 'She gave me a T shirt that said "One way to heaven" on it, and a combination padlock. I'll keep that lock, to lock her memory in my heart for ever. No one but me can undo the combination of that lock. She and I have secrets no one else shall ever know.'

Twink was so sure of God that her faith infected all who knew her, including children.

The third child was solemn, 'I went to say "Goodbye". She looked me straight in the eye. I think there were tears in her eyes as she said, "Don't let's say 'Goodbye' now, for there are no 'Goodbyes' for Christians." '

Twink could not possibly have known that she would never see us, her next-door-neighbours, again on earth. She could not know that four months after these parting words she

51

would be killed in a road accident, before those children returned again to their home in Thailand.

What made her travel all the way to Bangkok with her two little daughters to say her 'Goodbyes' to my husband and me when we went on leave? It was a fragrant memory that this family came to wave us off from the vicarage where we were staying before we left for the airport. She could not know that we would encase our last memory of her in our hearts and let it nestle there for ever; a serene madonna cradling a little girl on each arm, framed by hanging baskets of pink, lilac and yellow sprays of Thai orchids, her gleaming brown hair cascading to her shoulders, twinkle in eye, and song waiting to gently burst from her lips. The next time I stayed in that vicarage Twink had entered eternal rest. Twink who knew how to love others. Everyone was made to feel especially important to her. She and her little daughters deserved more than earthly treasures. These are of too little value to offer them. She left us all, suddenly in an accident, but in the acute ache of loss it was cold comfort to me to receive words which said she now received the riches she deserved. I was shattered by my own personal bereavement. We who love her want her alive. We want to see her, and not to have to imagine her in some unknown place.

The day after her death a preacher happened to preach on 'Blessed are those who mourn, for they will be comforted' (Matthew 5:4). Or, 'Blessed are you who weep now, for you will laugh' (Luke 4:21). Or to render it even more briefly, 'Happy are the unhappy'.

He had no way of knowing that someone suddenly bereaved would be listening to this one of a series of sermons.

I found it hard to listen to him. I did not want comfort, or laughter, or happiness. I wanted to continue the relationship I had had with Twink and the others, who had suddenly been snatched away.

Through a mist of tears such words of Jesus seemed totally preposterous. What was this parody about a father who apparently inflicts suffering upon his children and says it is a blessing to them? Could such terrible means ever justify so pathetic an end? 'Comfort, laughter, and happiness.' What are they when one so loved has gone? They barely warrant consideration. They are irrelevant.

The preacher continued. I wept unashamedly, desolated by

the seeming futility of these words. If he had offered me the numbness of anaesthesia I would have been grateful, for my feelings, raw from the previous day's deaths were too painful to derive solace from what I *thought* was being offered to me.

Perhaps similar circumstances evoke similar responses in some of us. We may be bereaved by actual death, or by the loss of one we had hoped to marry, or one whose friendship is a rich part of our lives.

Possible future happiness does not help us when we suffer in the present. Like any human being, I was hurt by loss. I was also deeply concerned because Bible promises about knowing God's comfort seemed to ring empty in my experience. When I needed to know God's comfort he seemed far away from me.

I had just begun to try to grasp the elements of New Testament Greek so that I could attempt to understand firsthand what the New Testament was communicating. The painful early weeks of grappling with the total unfamiliarity of this language bore sudden fruit. I found I had totally misunderstood this part of Jesus' teaching. I had taken the English translations at their face value; I had failed to consult any commentaries, for the teaching had seemed simple and uncomplicated, and so I had misinterpreted what Jesus was actually saying.

'Blessed are you that weep now, for you shall laugh' (Luke 6:21) did not mean that my human grief at bereavement could literally be interpreted as, 'Happy are the unhappy.' Therefore there was no need for me to force a smile, nor for me to be 'happy' or 'laughing' about what I experienced.

Study of the New Testament text revealed something quite different. To begin with, I had taken a sentence out of context. The meaning was only clear when Luke 6: 21 'Blessed are you who weep now, for you shall laugh' is read in its context and contrasted with the following verses: Luke 6:25, 'Woe to you who laugh now for you will mourn and weep'. Those about whom Jesus was speaking in verse 25 were those who were rebuked for their delusion and blindness to their need. They were complacently failing to mourn over their *spiritual poverty* and later would reap the results of their deluded apathy. Of course God is able to satisfy us completely and continually. Yet paradoxically this is only possible as we 'taste and see that the Lord is good', are satiated, and long for more. God is then able to lead us further on with him. When we are full we realise our emptiness, and how much more God can give us. This does not make human sense, nor is it logical, but it is not only a fact of Christian experience, it is contained in Jesus' teaching. So Jesus teaches that if we 'weep now' we 'shall laugh'.

The word 'weep' in Koine Greek, *klaio*, is one of the six words associated with grief and mourning, each carrying different shades of meaning. *Klaio* is not a gentle action. It is a violent emotion associated with grief. It is used in the New Testament for weeping at parting, and grief associated with death. We are told to 'weep with those who weep' with this intensity of feeling. Peter wept like this when he denied Christ, and similar tears of repentance marked the woman who anointed Jesus' feet. It is significant to note that *klaio* is never used when tears of joy are referred to.

Even as I write, memories of Twink enter the room through a song she introduced to me sung by a favourite of hers, Nana Maskouri, 'And I love you so . . . life began again the day you took my hand . . . the shadows fall on me . . . and yes I know how lonely life can be . . . ' Twink was one of those rare people whose gift for friendship was such that many of us felt unique and special to her. To lose her is to lose someone who made many of us feel of value and importance to someone.

Jesus allows me to weep for her, as I do two years later when memories stirred by associations that recall our friendship bring unbidden tears. 'Happy are the unhappy' leaves room for these tears for Twink because Jesus is speaking of a different kind of unhappiness.

The other record of similar words by Jesus is in Matthew 5:4; 'Blessed are they who mourn for they shall be comforted'. The word here for 'mourn' refers to sorrow in a general sense.

John Stott in *Christian Counter-Culture* suggests that these words do not refer primarily to those who mourn the loss of a loved one but rather to those who mourn the loss of their innocence, righteousness, and self-respect. It is a sorrow not of bereavement but of repentance. Not only is spiritual poverty acknowledged or confessed, but it is also mourned over in contrition.

Thus the comfort that is promised is the free forgiveness of God for those who are contrite. Consolation is personified in Jesus himself, the Messiah, who is to bind up the hearts of the broken hearted, and promises us the 'Comforter'.

Christ does this for us – yet we still mourn over the havoc of suffering and death which sin spreads throughout the world. For only in the final state of glory will Christ's comfort be complete. Only then will sin be no more, and 'God will wipe away every tear from their eyes.'[1]

The attitude of heart which Jesus is trying to teach us to adopt is found in James 4: 9, 10, 'Be wretched and mourn and weep. Let your laughter be turned to mourning and your joy to dejection. Humble yourselves before the Lord and he will exalt you.'

Laughter and tears, sorrow and joy, belong together as essential ingredients of our normal human emotional make-up. It is right for me to weep for those I love who have died. God does not promise me immunity from tears of grief.

Am I left comfortless?

At one stage when I felt lost in my grief I was staying in England in the small town of Olney. Bereavement in Thailand was followed a few months later by the death of my husband's father. The weeping willow trees bent low over the winding river. Their budding leaves drooped towards the water, picturing the tears I longed to release to be washed away in the sea of this world's grief. In this village William Cowper had lived, in sanity and in his moments of madness. Here he had gained and lost his faith. Here he had written the hymns that had enriched the world. The spire of the church where Cowper had worshipped rose magnificently, symbolically visible for miles around.

I turned under the willow trees to my companion, 'I can't think of Twink and the others as dead . . . '

'That's one of the strongest arguments for immortality,' was the thoughtful reply.

I lifted my eyes from the weeping trees to follow the church spire in its ascent towards the sky. In mourning I found comfort in the heritage of hope that is mine as a Christian. The buds on those trees were bursting with an Easter energy that spoke of life; life after death; the hope and belief that there really is life after death. In my natural human grief I am sustained by an assurance that resurrection after death is a fact. As I am human it is right for me to mourn as a human being. As I am a Christian it is right for me to hope with

55

the hope that is the gift given to each Christian.

In Oxford is a grave bearing the inscription, *Charles Williams. Poet. Under the mercy.* C. S. Lewis comments, 'No event has so corroborated my faith in the next world as Williams did simply by dying. When the idea of death and the idea of Williams thus met in my mind, it was the idea of death that was changed.'[2]

No one has so deepened my faith in life after death as Twink and my other friends did simply by dying. Now I believe that the theory I have known for years about the resurrection after death is true. They have died and now live an entirely different, but equally real life. Because they live this new life I am able to believe it is real for I know that they are real.

[1] *Christian Counter-Culture,*   John Stott.
[2] *Essays Presented To Charles Williams,*   C. S. Lewis (editor).

CHAPTER EIGHT

The joy of pain

Having offered to drive because my Thai friend was too scared to handle the wheel of the pick-up van I thought little more of my rash offer. She sensibly drove us out of the town so that her friends would not worry. Then she handed me the car keys. Within seconds I discovered that the handbrake was broken, the footbrake needed pumping, and one of the rear lights was out of action. The whole expedition was such an absurdity anyway that to go in any other kind of vehicle would have ruined the effect.

'Wait till late afternoon,' we were advised. 'They'll all be in the forest until then.'

Dusk was muffling the mountains when our odd party left the village: a fair haired English woman doctor, an Indian man with a degree in Oceanography who was an IVF staff worker, and a Thai woman graduate in Sanskrit. We headed off one of Thailand's better roads on to one of its worst. I am not sure that the track could be called a 'road'. The headman of the village at the point where the track ended owned a pick-up truck. He had hacked a road of sorts through the dense jungle which led endlessly upwards into the blue hills. I dared not shift out of first gear as the road twisted, serpent-like sideways and up and down in its precarious ascent.

'You drive well!' my Thai friend congratulated me.

'I need to after the accident at Manorom. After that I nearly hadn't the nerve to drive again,' I admitted. 'All I can say is that this car is safer in God's hands than in mine ... but I'll go on driving as carefully as I can.'

With aching backs and pounding heads we finally reached the Hmong tribal village for which we were heading. I was well aware of the fact that my predecessors, years ago, had trekked on foot to that village. Theirs was not even the comfort of an uncomfortable car journey.

Dusk was falling. We stood in the centre of the village, a clearing in dense jungle. Bamboo trees arched over the dry leaf roof of the nearest tiny house, built on stilts with only mats for walls. If the Family Planning Association was working here, no one was practising its teachings! Children abounded. Tiny tots carried even tinier creatures tied onto their backs. Mothers were working outside their houses, pounding maize, sorting the fruit collected from the forest that day, sifting tiny green beans from black baked pods.

The headman motioned us to enter his house. I went in and was momentarily blind in the thick blackness of the hut. After a few seconds I glimpsed light radiating from a small log fire over which some women were cooking the evening meal. Smoke stung my eyes. My vision was blurred by tears and the smoke haze. There were no windows. Corn cobs dangled from the rafters above my head. Cobwebs were countless.

My Thai friend, a city girl, enquired, 'No electricity?'

The headman looked up, surprised, 'No!' His tone indicated that there was really no need for such things.

By now my pupils had dilated and the shadowy forms which filled the room became human figures. I could see clearly that the house was jammed with people. Most were sitting on tiny benches a few inches off the hard-baked mud floor. A few chickens pecked, hungry and hopeful, in corners. A few bats hovered overhead, and darted at the small, locust-like insects on the walls.

Surely nothing beautiful came out of such darkness?

I was wrong. Two days later I visited another Hmong tribal village and saw the exquisite embroidery worked by these people. Such embroidery was worthy to be worn in palaces by queens. Yet were not these Hmong women, who were themselves beautiful, the queens of their race, and thus really the only ones entitled to wear such beauty? Minute patterns (perhaps comparable to the ancient tapestries preserved now in Versailles) were being worked painstakingly by this tribal group. In those dark, smoke-filled huts traditional art of rare beauty was being produced. Meanwhile the twentieth-century world (our world – not theirs which is the only real world to them) failed to notice their existence.

One of life's extreme paradoxes is that darkness can be a source of light. Pain may generate joy. Joy and pain partner one another in life's dance. We cannot appreciate one without experiencing the other. If we dull our senses by some opiate then we shall feel neither. To experience the depth of Christianity God intends us to experience, is to know the joy that only Jesus imparts. It involves opening ourselves up to the cost of following him: a price which is sometimes paid in pain.

To follow Jesus is not to obtain a panacea for this world's ills. The New Testament is clear. 'But we have this treasure in jars of clay to show that this all-surpassing power is from God and not from us. We are hard pressed on every side, but not crushed; perplexed, but not in despair; persecuted, but not abandoned; struck down but not destroyed. We always carry around in our body the death of Jesus, so that the life of Jesus may also be revealed in our body. For we who are alive are always being given over to death for Jesus' sake, so that his life may be revealed in our mortal body. So then, death is at work in us but life is at work in you' (2 Corinthians 4:7–12).

The supreme bereavement for many Christians is to be able no longer to sense God's presence and reality. Yet feelings of desolation, desertion, and distance from God are a common experience for many believers. We are led into a desert where our faith is so feeble that we wonder if it must inevitably be lost.

My delightfully unusual Thai friend led us on another expedition the next day. This time we bumped our way in the pick-up truck along a dirt track full of pot-holes, pigs and buffalo carts. We travelled on and on into the wilderness on a seemingly endless quest. My only comfort was that if there was a 'road' then it must go somewhere. But ahead lay only jungle and steep mountain cliffs.

Unexpectedly we jerked to a halt at a police check-point. 'They're only tourists!' My Thai friend pointed her chin at us and we were waved on.

We continued on our quest. There was still no sign of anything at the end of the road. A thorn from a twig scratched my face as it swept into the open car window. My thoughts were on what I was writing. 'Yes,' I wanted to exclaim, as I mopped the blood trickling down my face, 'sometimes God leads us to spiritual wastelands, and we can neither see him nor where he is taking us, and it hurts. Above all it hurts to be deprived of the sense of his presence,'

The sun was beating down, turning the truck into an oven as we persisted with our journey.

'We'll soon be there!' My Thai friend was far more optimistic than I was.

I was not reassured by the knowledge that in Thailand it is polite to tell people what you know they want to hear!

But she was correct. She slammed the footbrake on, and put the car into first gear to stop it from rolling backwards down the hill.

'Come on up!' she invited.

We clambered into a waiting jeep that carried us yet higher, like fledglings on the wings of a great bird, up the rough, unbelievably steep slope of the mountain.

At last we had arrived.

I stood in silent wonder.

We were high above the earth. We were higher than reality. Below us lay the plain, so far away that it was impossible to pick out roads or rivers. Far away in the distance lay mountain range tumbled upon mountain range, cascading in endless waves of blue-grey stone.

Behind us was an even more incredible sight. Perched like birds' nests upon a cliff nestled thousands of tiny wooden huts. We were welcomed, for my Thai friend lived with the owner of the shop from which these people bought petrol and stores.

I chatted in Thai to one man and to our joint surprise we found that his home village was only a few miles away from my home far away at Manorom. He had come here to make money.

'What are you doing?'

'I drive a tractor to level the earth for the tin miners,' he replied.

The ground was rough. I took off my rubber-thonged sandals and wandered barefoot along the narrow cliff paths, and swaying bridges of that mountain mining town. I had the feeling that Southend-on-Sea Town Council had taken its bathing huts, stripped off their paint, removed electricity and water, and then perched them on the side of this mountain as homes for these thousands. Yet a bathing hut was far too luxurious a comparison.

Poverty abounded, but not squalor. There was a disorganised organisation about this place.

Most of the men were underground, so we watched the women at work. They received the stones after the men had pounded them with their hammers. The stone had been hand-cut from the tin mines which some declared had been worked for over a hundred years.

These women were northern Thai beauties of whom one reads in tourist brochures but rarely encounters. Each squatted by a pool of mud, under a thatched roof placidly and gently scooping up the mud and patiently sifting it. Their transistor radios blared incongruous western pop songs as they worked. Each was beautiful, like a flower growing by a pool on the side of this unknown mountain. Who were these women, and what were they thinking? I wanted to know. When I talked to them they responded. Tourists did not come their way. They were anxious to show me the gain for their labour. They were proud of their handfuls of damp, brown-grey sand. They lived for that sand as long as they existed on the mountains. In this desolate place they sifted earth that contained 65 per cent tin mixed with it. They could sell the tin to the nearby factory.

My heart still lay in what I was writing, 'Out of this desolation comes tin. Out of tin comes that which is needed for life.' The lessons did not need to be spelled out letter by letter.

I could see Jesus on the cross in his agony and desolation, 'My God, my God, why have you forsaken me?'

I remembered the Bible words, 'But we see Jesus, who was made a little lower than the angels, now crowned with glory and honour because he suffered death, so that by the grace of God he might taste death for everyone. In bringing many sons to glory, it was fitting that God, for whom and through whom everything exists, should make the Pioneer of their salvation perfect through suffering' (Hebrews 2:9, 10).

God knows about the agony of desolation and promises us, 'Because he himself suffered when he was tempted, he is able to help those who are being tempted' (Hebrews 2:18).

I do not believe that suffering in any form is purposeless in the life of a Christian. I may never know the result of what has happened but I am confident that a price paid is never wasted. My problem is that I am confined to the limits of this world's time, and forget that God is acting in eternity. I want to see the result now (if not sooner) and am impatient when

I have to wait. Yet those women in the tin mines never see the end result of their hard work displayed in hardware shops; they never visit cities or see shops.

I know that nothing will diminish the awfulness of some realities, but I am assured that God can transmute evil into goodness. Sometimes I am allowed to see in retrospect how he has done this with situations in my own life. That this is possible is symbolised in the cross. The cross which man used when he carried out the greatest of all evils (the unjust murder of God's son) has become that which offers the greatest good to all mankind. Though I see no results I must not lose heart or abandon faith. An end result in future centuries cannot be seen with my myopic vision, limited only to my life-span.

When my children were younger I sometimes had to punish, correct, or instruct them. I find no anomaly in thinking that God, my Heavenly Father, needs at times to punish, correct or instruct his children. He may have to do this through the school of suffering. That he permits suffering in no way diminishes his love. I do not find it incongruous to think that sometimes his love is increased when he sees us suffer. It is harder to permit one you love to suffer than it is to allow someone for whom you feel indifference to suffer.

I am slow to grasp the full implications of John Donne's apparently simple words, 'No man is an island . . . ' It is hard to realise that the consequences of an evil act I commit may cause suffering for others in the tangled web of relationships involved in human existence. I am quick to say, 'God, why don't you stop them from doing that to me? They're hurting me!'

I am slow to realise that, by now, I might be unable to move any of my limbs, and be incapable of speech or sight if God paralysed each part of me every time I was about to act in a way that would hurt another person. Others are as human and fallible as I am, and they too have been given the gift of free will to use or misuse as I have. God is not always to blame for suffering encountered – man's misuse of his free will may be the cause. God is to be trusted that ultimately something of value will be produced.

The triumph of a song like Psalm 77 is produced as a result of suffering and a sense of spiritual desolation. The Psalmist can hardly be called an example of 'victorious Christian living' when he laments, 'I cried out . . . my soul refused to be comforted . . . my spirit grew faint . . . ' He has to remind himself that God's character does not change, and when he does this he bursts into a song of confidence in God. His suffering is not diminished but his psalm is the richer for the rediscovery of that which was lost.

Roads in the jungles of Thailand are worth exploring. The difficult journey is worth it in the end because something new is discovered which would have been missed otherwise. Life is richer and fuller. Suffering has meaning even if we do not know the purpose now, and only ever glimpse part of that meaning.

I was to learn many different personal lessons as a result of the road accident near Manorom. Different people learn different things. Personal bereavement was followed by a dull, aching sense of loss; loss of friends and, when I most needed him, apparent loss of God. In this spiritual wasteland God was able to communicate something precious to me.

Many people heard on the BBC that my husband had flown to Thailand. The telephone seemed to ring all day. I fell asleep that night cocooned by a new experience. I was wrapped in a blanket of love expressed by people many of whom I had previously not known. Many phoned to say, 'Our church prayed at all our services today for you all.'

One morning a week later I slipped on the third from bottom stair, fell, then went back to bed. I came round seven hours later to realise that it was afternoon and I must have been knocked out. I could see I had fractured my left wrist. I was swept up in a current of care by those in whose house we had been lent a flat, and was taken to hospital for manipulation of my wrist.

I chose to remain at home in case my husband phoned from Thailand, or my children, now back at boarding school, needed me.

Sleepless nights due to pain in my wrist merged with the sea of grief over bereavement. Above all I could not escape from a longing to talk to someone else who knew those I had loved and lost. Offers of hospitality from relatives and friends were not accepted. This pain and bereavement could only be shared with someone who knew both those who had died, and those who had been left to live at Manorom. Not having such a person, I chose solitude. Relatives and friends were powerless to help at this time.

In the days that followed I found that I was caught up in something far more beautiful than anything I had ever experienced before. Christians were deliberately going out of their way to help me bear my burdens. A tide of letters from friends and strangers engulfed me, so that within a week I had replied to over a hundred which said, 'We know, we care, we share.'

Five months earlier I had, in a small measure, 'wept with those who weep' in Burma as I visited that country as a tourist and shared joys and sorrows with Burmese Christian friends. News rapidly reached Burma through a tourist about the accident at Manorom. One of the first letters I received was one of comfort from a Christian I had grown to love in Burma. I had shared his family problems and cared about him and his family. Unexpectedly he heard my news, sensed my reactions and sorrow in solitude and wrote immediately. Some who had shared their own grief with me in the past were the first to write. Then followed a stream of letters from friends and strangers.

I longed to reply to these letters and acknowledge the love they expressed. Having a broken wrist I now found that others were moving in to help me in this frustrating helplessness. A Christian friend duplicated replies very quickly.

One day an unknown voice on the telephone asked, 'Do you need help addressing envelopes?'

'Yes!' I was perplexed.

'I'll be round this afternoon!'

The heaven-sent envelope addresser came unasked from the local church and went without me even knowing who she was. She left only a pile of envelopes addressed ready for posting. Other people came and folded letters, a difficult task one handed.

Someone else from the local church took me shopping to buy food that I could cook with one hand only. The daughter in the house in which we had a flat cleaned everything for me. One day I walked into the kitchen to find several days' washing-up neatly stacked clean on the table. I have never found out who did this for me.

Flowers arrived from a fellowship group in our home

church in London. Offers of transport, holiday accommodation, gifts of money, record and book tokens steadily trickled in.

I discovered new friends who were sensitive to my vulnerability in bereavement. God gave me the gift of caring Christians, who accepted me as I was; battered, bruised and bewildered.

Above all I was swept up into a new experience of being loved by my home church, All Souls, Langham Place, in London. I found that they cared in imaginative, loving ways. Friends and strangers from the church family phoned, wrote, and sent me flowers, money and even gifts for the family. People prayed as never before. My automatic reaction had been to 'run home' to the church as bereavement, and then injury hit me. The Rector was away but the congregation welcomed, and cared for me creatively. When I needed to stay in London they found me a quiet flat, and a physiotherapist appeared like magic twice a day to do all the things I could not do one-handed. Soon, my mother lovingly came to help, ignoring my odd bid for independence.

I found I was engulfed in a current from which I did not wish to escape. I was swept up in a tide of love coming from Christians, many of whom I had never met. I realised that the words spoken about the early church, 'See how these Christians love one another,' were being demonstrated in my church's attitude to me. I was the recipient of love. People were caring for me because they were demonstrating their love for the God they followed, by obeying his commands that his children should love one another.

This fresh facet of truth shone through the fog of feelings that God had deserted me in my extremity. I realised that God was caring for me through the love of his followers. No one has ever treated me with such imaginative care before, or if they have then I was not as sensitive to it as I now am. Had the Creator God prompted such creative caring? I was inclined to answer, 'Yes!'

In spiritual darkness and inability to feel God's reality, I discovered his love strong and dependable in the characters of Christians.

The action of my church was symbolised by the young woman who sat next to me one night when Manorom was being prayed for. She said nothing, but during the prayer put her strong arms round me and held me as a mother holds a child who is hurt.

Through the love of this church, and other Christians, God has shown me that he still loves me even in the wilderness of being unable to sense and respond to him. Other people were channels of God's love to me.

Jungle roads are dangerous and difficult to climb. Yet I experienced moments too precious to miss by not risking such trails. Enrichment and joy are part of life's rugged and painful paths. We will lose out if we cushion ourselves from life's painful experiences. We will lose the joy that God releases when pain and joy dance together in harmony. We will miss the enriching experiences God intends to give us, unless we are prepared to risk being hurt.

CHAPTER NINE

Indifference is easier

Had I really been like that?

My attitude seemed so uncaring and unlike Jesus that my immediate reaction was, 'Of course not. It's impossible!'

I lay spread-eagled on the vast expanse of a smooth lawn, on leave from Thailand in an English June heat wave. I basked in the beauty of creation, focused in particular on a single swan, silently drifting along a lake. I could not believe my reactions were as callous as they had been.

The scent of freshly mown grass and a shimmering haze hovering over the water tempted me to ignore reality and to allow my thoughts freedom to wander in pleasant pain-free paths of fantasy. Yet I was unable to escape uncomfortable home truths.

The truth I would prefer to ignore is that I have neighbours, and I have not cared much for them. Sometimes I have not really cared at all. I do not need to study the story Jesus told about the man who was beaten up on the road between Jerusalem and Jericho, or to question Jesus, 'Who is my neighbour?'

I know perfectly well that anyone in need is a person to whom I should open my heart in love and compassion. The troublesome truth which nags like toothache is that often I am more preoccupied with myself than with other people. So people are neglected.

On that particular day I had reached a point where I almost prayed, 'Lord, please don't show me any more people with any more needs, because I can't help anyone any more. Please leave me alone to look after myself for a little while.'

This facet of myself that loves itself so much was made clear to me as I learned about India, and in particular about Calcutta, through friends who have made this city real to me. I always thought I cared, but the more I learned, the more I realised how superficial my concern had been. I suppose I could not have cared less, and I know I should have cared more.

Two pebbles nestle on cotton wool in my living room. They were picked up from the streets of Calcutta and given to me to help me to remember. As I handle the two rough stones, and read the familiar handwriting addressed to me I cannot excuse myself and say, 'Calcutta is only a place which exists on the television, about as real as Disney Land in a nightmare – so forget it!'

Calcutta is for real.

Words from a friend's letter show me just how real Calcutta is. She is a city about which I cannot be indifferent.

'I have met today those who have shown me that Calcutta is a city of saints as well as of slums.

'Vijayan Pavani founded the Calcutta Samaritans when he put his own phone number in the newspaper inviting any in distress to ring him. Thirty-eight phoned him that day . . . I cannot convey the strength, depth and pity of this man. Nor can I easily write of his gentle wife and enchanting children . . . In addition to all he does as Director of the Samaritans, he gives himself to a whole range of urgent and heart-rending causes in the city – half-way homes for alcoholics, after-care for prisoners, work among the one-third of Calcutta's students who are on drugs.'

In 1979, I met Vijayan and his family myself in Calcutta and knew my friend had told me the truth. I could identify with many other things my friend had said, for I too visited the same places in 1979. The letters continue,

'I saw the famous picture of Christ on the cross over Calcutta and the words, "Seeing the city he wept over it." '

When I left Calcutta after my brief visit I had to weep over all that the city had shown me. My friend continues,

'Outside the cathedral is a nativity scene. Mary, Joseph, the Child, shepherds, etc. – the usual thing except it is set in one of the sewage pipes in which so many in Calcutta still sleep.

'Our other contacts in Calcutta were Pastor and Mrs David Lamb (Chinese from China) who for thirty years have worked twenty hours a day among the Chinese and through them, and among many others in the city. I have never met a more fervent man, a man overflowing with tides of goodwill to all mankind. He and his wife swept us up into a cyclone of welcome.

'Vijayan and the Lambs filled our day. Briefly we walked the streets. They are as you expect. Except that you perhaps have not expected to see so many who are not in rags; Calcutta is a colourful city, many of its millions live adequately, and apparently with some enjoyment. But there is the Calcutta we know about. Humanity feeding like rats on garbage, the limbless sitting on the pavement, a claw reaching out for your charity. So many, so lost, that who will notice or care if one dies?

'Perhaps it is only very early (for this I have not seen), or very late in the day (this I have seen) when thousands sleep on the pavement, that you see the full tragedy of Calcutta.

'Pastor and Mrs Lamb, like Vijayan, like Mother Theresa, like all the saints of Calcutta, are doing something about *today's* suffering . . .

'We were taken to Tangra, slum of slums in this wretched city. Mrs Lamb showed me a Billy Graham calendar – and the words well worn – as we edged our way through the filth, "I will never leave you nor forsake you."

'Tangra is the tannery area of Calcutta – and those who deal in animal skins are the most despised of the sunken silt of humanity in which Calcutta sprawls. The Lambs have built a church here. We slipped in briefly and heard some children sing. They had built a school, which as well as teaching these deprived little ones, both clothes and feeds them.

'The destitution of Tangra is something which even my opaque eyes notice. I think it is better that you are not here, because I believe it would have broken your heart.

' . . . eventually we found our way back to this quiet haven, and I crept under the mosquito netting, deeply troubled by the contradictions of the day, the contradictions of the city . . . Vijayan and his wife, Pastor and Mrs David Lamb witness both to a love that will not be resisted and also to an ultimate optimism. Those who live and die on the streets, or in the stinking shanties off the streets, and who have done so since India was born, epitomise ultimate pessimism.'

I am shaken back to reality for as I write in an English June, jets fly overhead towards Heathrow Airport. All I read is for real. As I write, the summer cuckoo calls me away to dream land, but overhead the jets crash through the sky, reminding me that Calcutta must not be ignored. Calcutta, and all she represents, is my neighbour; to be forgotten, or given a few pounds to clear my conscience, or to be a city I can learn to love truly as Jesus has taught me to love my neighbour as myself.

In 1979 I met Mother Theresa myself and found everything to be as my friend has described it; 'Mother Theresa's Home of the Dying Destitute is almost exactly as you have so often pictured it. You walk into it (as I have said we would walk into heaven) with a sense, not of surprise but of recognition, the awareness that you knew all along that it would be like this.

'You step into it from a corner of a square in the teeming bazaar, the cows, the cheap stalls, the pavement shelters, the noise, the smells, the wretched ragged of Calcutta squatting placidly, waiting for nothing. You hardly notice the entrance, set between two cheap stalls.

'You just walk in – no door, turn a corner, and you are there in the rooms you know so well, one for the men, one for the women; bare, clean, cool, bathed in the light that is sometimes lent to a lovely church by fine glass – though no such splendours here. Just rows of low beds, pallets on the floor; light, silent, peaceful. The destitute, dying in peace. The sisters move quietly among them, but they stop and chat to us, relaxed, serenely accepting without question our gratuitous visit. There are children playing at the end of the ward. It's all so still. No one seems in pain, though many are very near to death. By the door a young American holds the hand of an emaciated figure almost, I judged, almost dead.

'I slip away from the others. I go and sit with one or two of those who have come here to die. I hold their hands, try by simple truth, by an embrace, to convey your love to them. Some are nearly dead, others are dying, but while they die, they live and talk quietly to each other. It is a house from which all fear has been banished. Love surrounds, supports, succours those who find at last, after who knows what griefs and pains, a peace in death that life never gave them. It is the

70

loveliest house I have ever entered, and if I am not changed by it then I am indeed lost. All you have read about it is true. Just as we were leaving a barely breathing creature of skin and bone was carried in.

'Nothing else in the day could be quite as important . . . so I have been to Calcutta for you.'

And in 1979, when I went to Calcutta for myself, I found my reactions were the same as my friends;

'There is the intolerable burden imposed by the paradoxes of Calcutta – Mother Theresa with the goddess Kali's temple next door, the selfless saints and the stinking cities . . . how dare I go on brooding on my boring little troubles when Calcutta is Calcutta, and the sisters still move so quietly between the dying?'

I read no further. There is no need. I put the letter aside.

I am left with no excuse. Not only do I know from correspondence but I know from my own visits that the tragedy that is Calcutta is not part of a television documentary film that will disappear when I change TV channels at the push of a button. The easy way out is to ignore everything which it is hurtful to acknowledge. It is easy to pretend that Calcutta (and all that she represents) and the daily suffering in different parts of the world do not really exist. News today but gone tomorrow.

As I write the cuckoo still calls, encouraging me to turn my thoughts to the beauty of the English summer. But again the call is drowned by a jet plane screaming through the sky, shrieking, 'I've been to Calcutta! What you hear and read is real – don't ignore it! Remember, you've been there yourself!'

The temptation to apathy is attractive, 'You've had your share of suffering, now have a break and forget it. Go and lie in the sunshine and get sunburnt!'

It seems that half of England is pouring down the road a few hundred yards away in the summer heat wave – car roofs open, sun-tan lotion drenches fair skins, and a festive spirit filling the air.

'Forget, go and relax!' I am tempted.

Yet, today is a day for remembering and not a day for forgetting.

Now the idea of spending the day attempting to fry my fair skin brown seems wrong. God loved and give his only

Son. Do I care so little that I can go and lie in the sun and dream? While I dream millions die. There are things I could be doing to help some of these millions whom I don't know. Today is a day to care.

To be God's child and to follow him is to venture, if I am willing, into the unknown and costly path of caring for others. I cannot possibly love as he loves. At the highest I can perhaps endeavour to reflect a little of his love to those who are loveless. To theorise is easy, but to turn theory to action is difficult. How can I, who have worked in the past as a doctor in up-country Thailand, and am now living as a British housewife, care for those in the rest of the world who are in desperate need? God loves the *world*, and somehow he must fill me with his love, so that I too can learn to reflect his love.

I must not, dare not, allow glimpses of Calcutta to pass me by without impressing me and changing my life.

Apathy is a luxury in which I dare not indulge.

CHAPTER TEN

The quality of love is not strained

A N INNER imperative sometimes leads me to act automatically.

One day in 1979 I was on duty at Manorom hospital. Six children under five were in-patients, paralysed with the virulent poliomyelitis virus, ravaging young lives in some areas of Thailand.

Two of these tiny beauties were my patients. Being a mother as well as a doctor I faced emotional conflicts in treating them, for they represent what my children were in a bygone era before adolescence stole infancy and innocence from them.

I fought despite the frustration of knowing my fight could be futile; my battle was the fight against masterly inactivity. Old grannies chewing betel nut had to be persuaded that their persistent massage of paralysed limbs would lead to worse damage, contrary to their ancient teaching and beliefs. Anxious relatives begging for injections had to be convinced that any injected limb might face future paralysis. This went against attempts to educate country people that injections were not to be feared but welcomed.

I watched a three-year-old girl I came to love lying motionless, her trusting brown eyes meeting mine in silent confidence that seemed to communicate a conviction that I would save her. I hardened my heart when paralysis crept up from her legs to her arms. By now her father had confided in me that her youngest sister had died at home the previous week from the same disease. By the time the child was unconscious and having difficulty with breathing I had come to identify with her family. When she stopped breathing and her tiny heart stopped fluttering I helped wrap the white shroud around her resting, quiescent body.

Her grandmother wept on the floor, thankfully clinging to

my body and gaining support from my arms tight round her.

I had tried to do something to stop the death of this child, for I find that to encounter suffering in the world is to face the challenge to attempt to right it. I knew there was more I must do. When the family was calm again I called them to me,

'How many little children are there at home?'

Granny responded, 'Five.'

'Then bring them tomorrow for polio vaccine.'

By the end of the following day I did not know whether to weep with helpless laughter or to hide my red embarrassed face in a cool pool in the flooded rice fields. The previous night at the child's cremation in the Buddhist monastery, the abbot had decreed over a loudspeaker system that all children under thirteen years of age were to go straight to Manorom at dawn the next day. Three lorries were hired and filled with children. They bumped across dusty rice fields, on to a brown all-weather road and across the river on the ferry. Then, 150 children and their relatives were disgorged on to the grass in front of the hospital so that Friday midday looked like Monday morning in the out-patient department of the hospital.

To laugh or weep? My pronouncement about preventive medicine had never been proclaimed at funerals by Buddhist monks before, and had never ever been so dramatically effective. By lunchtime the hospital stocks of polio vaccine were non-existent and the pharmacist went off on his motor-bike to beg or borrow from the neighbouring towns. When he returned at 4 p.m. many of the children had given up hope and gone home. They had returned to a village from which six children had died of poliomyelitis in the last ten days. Would more of them be paralysed for life or die needlessly? To know is to care. To care is often to be impelled to act. Our actions may not succeed. I believe that what is important is whether we did all we possibly could rather than whether or not our attempts produced the desired result. We can do no more than try our hardest.

Some of us must come to terms with these words, ' "Lord, when did we see you hungry and feed you, or thirsty and give you something to drink? When did we see you a stranger and invite you in, or needing clothes and clothe you? When did we see you sick or in prison and go to visit you?"

'The King will reply, "I tell you the truth, whatever you

did for one of the least of these brothers of mine, you did for me" ' (Matthew 25: 37-40).

Our neighbour may be understood as anyone who comes to us in any need. Unknowingly he comes as Christ's representative in Christ's name, to receive from us the love and service we long to give to Christ himself. In this neighbour we serve Christ. As a doctor this is one of the many ways in which I may regard my patients: especially when more is demanded of me than I am obliged to offer.

William Barclay clarifies one way of interpreting Jesus' words in Matthew 25 when he says that this 'shows us that the standard of the final judgement will be quite simply, "Were you concerned about this bit of trouble or not? . . . " The church is the Body of Christ. That phrase may mean many things, but it means one simple and practical thing. Jesus is no longer here in the body. He is here in the Spirit. But that means that if something is to be done, he has to get a man or woman to do it for him. Nothing can teach a man or a woman (about God's love) unless God's children will do it. The help which he wishes to lavish on the aged, the weak, the suffering, the sorrowing, must come through human beings. He needs men to be hands for him; men to speak for him; feet to run his errands . . .'[1]

A man is made up of many different facets. God's outgoing selfless love must reach every part of him. Man must never be thought of only as 'a soul to be won for Christ'. Humans are to be loved as whole people. Today some of us verge on the extreme of loving the physical and emotional man to the exclusion of his spiritual nature.

Mother Theresa reminds us, 'The biggest disease of today is not leprosy or T.B., but rather the feeling of being unwanted, uncared for, and deserted by everybody. The greatest evil is the lack of love and charity, and the terrible indifference towards one's neighbour, who lives at the roadside assaulted by exploitation, corruption, poverty and disease.'

To care we must be aware. We need to notice those who have needs which never hit newspaper headlines. When major tragedy strikes, then we may be moved to act. Yet, when a mother grinds slowly through life, crushed by domestic trivia; when a commuter sinks in a sea of depression; or when a daughter's out-of-work hours are totally absorbed in caring for a dependent relative, then do we even notice, let alone care? Do we care enough to try and help? Such people face problems which are as important as the acute need of major disasters.

Christ comes to us through those in need. Do we see him? He may come to us in some people for whom we feel immediate instinctive antipathy. We know that barriers such as race and class do not exist for God. It is not necessary for us to approve of someone's actions in order to love him. We may not like a person, we may disagree with his opinions and the things he does, but God calls us to exert our wills to practise a love which reflects his, and unconditionally accepts others.

Incredibly we are called to exercise a quality of love which seems humanly impossible. We are confronted by the example of a good and holy man who never acted in any way that was not totally loving. He was cruelly killed like those criminals of his ancient culture who underwent the death penalty. He knew that his trial was unjust. As he died, slowly and painfully, acutely aware of his spiritual isolation, he prayed aloud that those who killed him in such a manner should be forgiven and not punished by God.

When Jesus commands I am prepared to give more weight to his words than I would to other people's for he has practised what he preached, ' "I tell you, love your enemies and pray for those who persecute you" ' (Matthew 5: 44).

It is trite but true to say that we can hate sin but love the sinner. Perhaps we can identify and then hate the thing within a person, that makes him an enemy (or a person we dislike), and yet love the person himself. If love involves actions rather than emotions we can set our wills to desire the highest good for all men, including those people we dislike.

How do I react when someone digs an emotional or verbal knife into me? Automatically I want to fight back bitterly and to hurt as much – or more – as I have been hurt. Yet Jesus indicates that his children are to follow a different behaviour pattern – one that can only be theirs if he is allowed to change and control them.

The correspondence columns of 'Christian' magazines, or Christian coffee break gossip, reveal the sad truth that we who are called to love, exert time and energy subtly hurting and destroying one another. We look at someone who has apparently done wrong and smugly feel, 'I'm better than he is. I've never said or done such a thing.'

Is this Jesus' way of love?

Sometimes we need to be more sensitive to those who are potential casualties in what appears to us to be the mere trivia of living. As we read reports, minutes of committee meeings, articles, letters, book reviews, we may begin to sense that someone will learn a necessary lesson, but that that person may be hurt in the process. Perhaps he must learn, but can we love him through this time of hurting? I believe that sometimes Jesus wants us to act remedially in such situations with a word of loving, positive affirmation to the person involved. His sense of value as a person can be strengthened through something as small as a telephone call, a postcard, or even by our sitting next to him in the coffee-break. It is easier to write letters to the editor than it is to read letters to the editor and then pen a few words to the person under criticism – words which imply that God's love is unfailing towards everyone.

To love is to be sensitive to people whose position makes them vulnerable to hurt. To love is not to acquiesce or agree with that for which they are being criticised. It is loving to show them that they are of personal worth to you, and so to God their Father. Their actions, words, or beliefs are for the moment immaterial. In an extreme case, a small loving gesture may save me from the desperation of despair and self worthlessness that leads to suicide. Simply to know that some-one somewhere, knows and cares whether I am alive or dead may sometimes be very important: and such knowledge need cost only a postcard.

What about the lonely singles and the elderly and those isolated in the solitude of positions of leadership? The highest and lowest are equal in Jesus' eyes; should they not be so in ours? Is an archbishop really of more value as a human being under the shadow of Calvary than his window cleaner? Does anyone make his window cleaner feel that he is a person of significance to God or not? Is he *only* a window cleaner? No! Surely, with the archbishop he is a person of supreme and precious significance to the God who loves him infinitely. Status, colour and creed get lost as we learn how to love. If we can learn to love as individuals, then as churches, we may reach whole groups whom we perhaps find it difficult to love naturally; immigrant communities, and others who feel cut off from society. Surely all men must be made to feel that we and our churches love them, and naturally absorb them into all parts of life where we meet as fellow human beings. As long as we allow people to feel they are cut off from us we are failing to love as we should.

The attitudes which some people express about immigrants make me angry.

I have lived in another country for fifteen years as an immigrant myself, although I have gone as a missionary to that land. In Thailand, Thai Buddhists have often lavished on me the kind of loving I long to see Christians offer to those who are strangers and foreigners in England. Often in moments of grief or loneliness in Thailand, a Thai friend or acquaintance had spotted my need. When I have been working in the hospital, with my children thousands of miles away at school in England, and my husband away in Bangkok on business, a Thai woman has offered to spend the night with me so that I should not be alone. At such times the night watchman has given me coconuts and bananas, and a Thai nurse has placed a single red rose in a vase on the hospital consulting room desk. Many times in small ways Thai Christians and Buddhists alike have loved me and have not been too busy to notice that I was alone and that I appreciated such sympathy and loving gestures.

I am ashamed at the way my homeland has sometimes treated my Thai friends when they have gone to study or work there. Some, but not many people offer the generous hospitality that the poorest person in the Third World offers to strangers. Do my Asian friends wonder why such wealthy Westerners treat them as if they are unimportant (for to them the stranger and foreigner is an honoured guest)? They are too courteous to ask me.

Many years ago in a lonely missionary situation, when my husband and I were sometimes urgently needed simultaneously at work, my Thai next-door-neighbour assumed that it was her duty to care for my children. She was a busy teacher, but several times she looked after my children on her only day off work. Whenever my husband was called to the hospital at night, in that same isolated situation, my other next-door-neighbour's husband used to sit up guarding our house until my husband returned. I was unaware until the day we left that village that he had lost sleep for so many nights because of his concern for me. I discovered from such non-Christians that I am still at kindergarten in the school of learning to care.

I believe we are called to care for those who silently suffer emotionally. The depth of their suffering is unknown and unimaginable. Many wear a mask to hide their grief from the world. Outwardly all is well. Inwardly the fires of Gehenna may slowly burn in searing, slow torture, day and night. We may need to direct someone with psychological needs to a qualified counsellor, or to a doctor who can refer that person for psychiatric help where necessary. Yet we cannot totally pass the buck to those who are paid in their profession to care for those with psychological needs. When that person is away from a professional helper (most of the time) dare we care enough to stand alongside on the depths of the pit where they stand, and offer a supportive heart and hand? If we dare, then let's face it now, we will often be badly hurt ourselves. Those with psychological needs often hurt professional or other helpers. Are we willing to be hurt? Are we willing to be very badly hurt? Can we look Jesus straight in the eye and say, 'No, Lord! Even for you I cannot do this'?

I had a penfriend who developed a mental illness. She wrote fourteen-page letters which were barely legible and often incomprehensible. Yet through this correspondence I learnt to love the spirit of one whom I had never met but knew spiritually as a beautiful, sensitive and caring person. We learned to be concerned for each other. I was at a loss to know how to reply to her letters. She was receiving both psychiatric help and counselling from her experienced and caring minister. In the end I sent cards from Thailand to England that were intended to convey one message only in as many ways as I could create, 'I know you are alive, I care, and I appreciate you.' I bought a collection of beautiful cards and tried to send them to her regularly.

When she committed suicide, I found I had come to love this person I had never met and that her death affected me deeply. I was strangely moved that one of her few close friends should write and tell me that she was dead, so that I knew before my last letter to her was returned by her solicitor with one enigmatic word on it 'deceased'. I was overwhelmed when her friend told me how much I had meant to this woman

79

whose illness had led her to take her life. Our relationship by post had been special enough for this friend to write to me, a stranger.

I learned that to care for someone with emotional needs is costly in many ways. This friendship led me to despair and helplessness as I faced unexpected bereavement. I floundered in bewildered hurt at the death of somebody I had never met.

There is no end to loving other people once we are aware of the possibilities.

We are to love those who are given to us regardless of our likes, preferences, or convenience. Why? Because Jesus wants to express his love through us, and because we can love other people as Jesus' representatives.

[1] *Gospel of Matthew*,   William Barclay.

CHAPTER ELEVEN

The strain of loving

SOME of us will identify with Monica Furlong when she writes, 'I seem to be worse at loving my neighbour than almost anyone else I have ever known . . . ' and goes on to express her reactions, 'If I'm so sensitive on this subject, it is because I have just been reading one of those books which says that the Christian home should be a perpetual refuge to the stranger – the door ever open to the alien and the unloved, the coffee pot always on the stove, hospitality constantly available with a listening ear and an understanding heart. *That*, says the book, is how to love one's neighbour – a kind of domestic version of overseas aid. In addition, one should be busy helping the needy and infirm who live round about one . . . perpetual busyness, the constant presence of others, endless demands on my interest and sympathy, would quite simply drive me barmy, in a way that the extrovert end of Christian practice always finds it so hard to believe.'[1]

These are no idle words. Jesus gives us two commandments, to love God and to love our neighbour as ourselves. Some of us manage to swing to one extreme and become so immersed in our world and the demands that people make on us that there is never any time for God (and church services may not be really 'God time', for 'church' may be the time we spend in preoccupation with our own troubles and the troubles of others).

We *say* 'I love God in my neighbour' but this can be a subtle disguise of the fact that we think little about God in reality. Our own and our neighbours' needs consume our resources of time and energy, stretching us to our limits. Someone else's need of us makes us feel wanted and of significance to someone in this impersonal world. Gradually and unconsciously we may derive strength from the fact that we are significant because we are needed. Our original motive, to love our neighbour for Jesus' sake, or to love Jesus in our neighbour, is forgotten. It may not always be wrong for some of us to need to be of significance to someone. This motive for service has produced notable people who have changed the lives of countless people who were helpless before. However, we need to be wary on this point. Things can go very wrong if we become dependent on a person and his need of us to find significance in our lives. Excessive dependence of this kind leads to a frightening bereavement when such relationships are ended. It is good from time to time to assess our motives in caring relationships. That which once was pure and good can turn sour, restrictive and harmful, if exclusiveness develops. As Christians, our original motive in forming caring relationships may have been extended from the desire only to express *agape* love, but in the end, due to our own lack of sensitivity, our stupidity or selfishness we may be sucking dry those whose lives we would fill with God's love.

Of course this can occur in the family unit. Parents love their children, give their lives to them for years, and often find satisfaction in needing to be needed. In a relationship where a parent depends on his or her children for significance the crunch comes when the children leave home, or the adolescent defiantly shouts, 'I'm me! I don't need you any more!'

The adult who has been sustained by a child's need of him is bereft suddenly of the only thing which gave significance to his life. He is bewildered and shattered. He may become bitter and resentful, and with confused emotions try to hurt the one he loves who has hurt him.

The tragedy is manifest by the fact that no one understands why everyone is suddenly hurting everyone else. The answer is too simple to face. While the child has become independent, the dependent adult cannot now face life alone.

Perhaps one of the greatest gifts we can give to those we love is the gift of freedom when the time has come that we are no longer needed. To set free those we love may require more unselfishness than to lavish love on them unstintingly. Years of loving and caring will have created deep bonds. Roots have sunk deep into our personalities. We have seen in a person that which is precious and beautiful even when they have felt worthless; together we have weathered the storms, we have laughed, wept and shared, and spun a web of mutual confidence in which we feel secure to reveal our innermost beings.

Such relationships are so rare and precious that we treasure them more than anything else. We long for them to remain for the duration of our lives. Yet for the sake of all concerned, sometimes such close ties within and without our family, have to be severed. Freedom must be offered for each to go his own way, or to decide to stay together. Jesus' love was never selfish. We only pretend to love if we deny others the freedom to an independence that will set them on the road to learning to live without us. We want to be wanted, but this is selfish and not self-giving love. A painful lesson for the parents, children, and close friends to learn.

I find that this business of 'loving my neighbour' involves much more than a jolly, hearty, open home, open ear policy. Most important, it involves loving God to the extent that his love can reach through me to unlikely, cobwebby corners of the world.

How can God's self-giving love be channelled through me if I do not give God time to work on and in me to show me how to love? I need time to 'vegetate' – as Thomas Merton calls this activity. I need to take time out of a life full of people with endless needs, just to be alone and simply to be.

To be what? To be nothing. Just to be. Just to sit quietly and to allow God to soak into my being and begin to sort me out. I must force myself to make, or to take, time for this. I need to recognise that allowing myself regular periods of such apparent inactivity is the only way in which I can live the active life I so enjoy. Hours or days of inactivity in God's presence are necessary if I am to love my neighbour. I need to thicken my skin when others accuse me of laziness. I am answerable to God on this score.

In solitude I am able to understand what Jesus is really commanding me to do in my life and situation.

C. S. Lewis helps me to begin to understand this, as he describes the *agape* or 'gift love' that the New Testament commands as opposed to need love; 'This primal love is gift love . . . God who needs nothing, loves into existence wholly superfluous creatures in order that he may love and perfect them . . . he communicates to men a share of his own gift love. This is different from the gift loves he has built into their natures. These never quite simply seek the good of the loved object for the object's own sake . . . But divine gift love: love himself working in a man, is wholly disinterested and desires what is simply best for the beloved. Again, natural gift love is always directed to objects which the lover finds in some way intrinsically lovable – objects to which affection, or eros, or a shared point of view attracts him . . . But Divine gift love in the man enables him to love that which is not naturally lovable . . .'[2]

In daily living we find that true *agape* love means that we strive for an almost impossible goal. No matter what another man does to us we will never, under any circumstances, seek anything but his good (read that sentence again . . . even as I write it, I am appalled as I begin to imagine the many situations where I could not begin to practise what I am writing). We must deliberately set our wills in that direction. Loving has now become a matter of the will rather than the emotions.

When the gossip grapevine or 'gripe vein', as a Swiss friend aptly calls it, passes round a story involving me, and I know the source of that story, then I could easily react in a way that would harm the one who started it. I can choose whether or not to retaliate. The practice of *agape* love implies that I should try to do nothing but that which will bring good for others, even those who hurt me.

I do not see this as being a passive, doormat type of Christian over whom all may trample, leaving muddy, critical footsteps which no one bothers to clear up. Rather, I see it as a version of 'turning the other cheek', as Jesus commanded us. I would like to say nothing, but try in attitude to express the feeling, 'You have hurt me so much that I have deliberately set my will to seek nothing but your highest good. God knows I'm human and want to bash your head against a brick wall. He is going to have to show me what to do to give me the strength to love you. I hate your guts. I hate what you have done to me. Only Jesus can make me love you, and I will trust him to change my ugly attitude.'

I glimpse a manner of loving I covet: 'Love means a refusal to see, think of, or deal with one's neighbour except in the light of what Christ has done for him; as a brother for whom Christ died,'[3] as C. E. B. Cranfield defines it in *A Theological Word Book of the Bible*.

What a standard! How different from the sloppy slush that goes under the name of 'love'!

I begin to see also that it is not preposterous for Jesus to *command* me to love. No one can command me to exercise an *emotion.* However, I can be commanded to set my will to allow my actions to be based on certain motives. When Jesus commands me to love, he has commanded me to set my will so that I will act in a way that promotes only the highest good for another person (my own likes or dislikes are not particularly relevant. It helps if I like, for my part is then more comfortable). I can choose to obey or disobey Jesus' command to love. Therefore the problem of loving those I cannot like ceases to be a real problem. I can get on and act and leave God to sort out my emotions as time passes.

As I stagger under the realisation that I cannot evade the command 'Love your neighbour as yourself' by saying, 'But I don't even like him, so please may I be excused?' I am knocked out by a final, under-the-chin blow; the knowledge that I am unable to obey such an impossibly demanding command. As the count out goes from ten to one, I realise, coming to full consciousness, that I cannot begin to obey *alone.* I raise my head in shame, for it is made plain in the New Testament that I am not expected to love others by any solitary effort.

The Bible says, 'I have been crucified with Christ and I no longer live, but Christ lives in me. The life I live in the body, I live by faith in the Son of God who loved me and gave himself for me' (Galatians 2:20). And 'The fruit of the Spirit is love, joy, peace, patience, kindness, goodness, faithfulness, gentleness, self-control. Against such things there is no law' (Galatians 5:22, 23). And 'Since we live by the Spirit, let us keep in step with the Spirit. Let us not become conceited, provoking and envying each other' (Galatians 5:25, 26).

C. S. Lewis comments, 'While natural man has some selfish love that desires the best for others and acts accordingly, this can only grow to a maximum in any individual by a supernatural infusion of gift love that comes from a prior relationship with God, through Christ.'[2]

I find from the *Theological Word Book* that Martin Luther gives an illustration of this which makes immediate sense to me: 'A man is placed between God and his neighbour as a medium, which receives from above and gives out again below, and is like a vessel or a tube through which a stream of divine blessing must flow without intermission to other people.'[3]

Christian *agape* love is, as Monica Furlong hinted in words quoted at the beginning of this chapter, far more than busy, 'Christian do-gooding'.

We must remember the importance of putting our relationship with God first as we seek to serve him. Then we must remember that to love as a Christian is an exercise of the will, and at the same time begin to grasp the amazing truth that we are to be like water pipes through which the Holy Spirit can express the living water of his love for men.

This assumes that our lives are not so busy that God is squashed out. It assumes we are giving God time to percolate our personalities to make our loving a mirror of his self-giving love.

[1] *Contemporary Christianity*,   Monica Furlong.
[2] *The Four Loves*,   C. S. Lewis.
[3] *A Theological Word Book of the Bible*,   Alan Richards (editor).

CHAPTER TWELVE

Strains that threaten to break

To begin to learn to 'love our neighbour as ourselves' and to 'bear one another's burdens' is costly. Let no one deceive us that true loving will not exhaust us to the limit.

We are challenged in the New Testament to 'carry each other's burdens and in this way you will fulfil the law of Christ' (Galatians 6:2).

As we read these words we must read them in their context and not isolate them so that their meaning is distorted. If we read the preceding part of the chapter we see that these words follow a call to us to restore gently and to reinstate anyone who is obviously disobeying Christ. We are to share the failure and guilt that he may be carrying. Of course guilt cannot be totally shared with anyone else, as is clear from the succeeding words, 'For each one should carry his own load' (Galatians 6:5).

To be involved in the life of another at any depth is hard. Superficial relationships are easy and they are often right. The privacy of another's personality must be respected. No door should be hacked open with psychological hatchets. It is not for us ruthlessly to break down a door of discretion, enter the secret depths of a person's life, and then find, when it is too late, that we have permanently scarred that person by our blundering, bulldozing interference. We should have kept out and left well alone.

On the other hand, occasionally we encounter someone who opens their inner heart a crack. Before we back away from them we need to be sensitive to the fact that they may be begging us, 'Come in . . . No one has been in here before. I must show someone who I really am. I need to see if you find me, in my rottenness, acceptable or not.'

Some of us find it a problem to know how far to go in seeking to understand another person. We are not trained in psychiatry and we are venturing into the pastures of this discipline. A point must come when we say, 'I have shared your burden of failure. I have seen some of the dark corners of your life. I love you and I accept you. I shall go on loving you. But now we must stop wallowing in your dark hole and get up and live.'

As we learn to love deeply we will find it costs everything we have and are, and Jesus' words take on fresh relevance, ' "My command is this: love each other as I have loved you. Greater love has no one than this, that one lay down his life for his friends. You are my friends if you do what I command" ' (John 15:12–14).

At some time or other we will find that caring means we have to come to terms with our limitations as human beings. We may long to love and give ourselves totally in a situation of need but be forced to say, 'No'.

'No' is a word we must not be afraid to use when we are sure it should be said.

We need to take stock of ourselves, of those around us, and especially of our families, to see what the expenditure of ourselves in caring for others is costing those most closely involved in our lives. Are we caring for others at the expense of those who are dependent on us? We need to assess our priorities carefully.

How right of a certain businessman to question me about how much he should expect himself to bear others' burdens. He is a gentle, artistic, sensitive man who expends emotional energy in his job, seeking to communicate Christ through audio-visual means. All day long he pours himself out in creative activity. He is exhausted by the end of a working day. He is a commuter, leaving at 6.30 a.m. and arriving home at 7 p.m. Such a man has very few hours left for his family. Perhaps God is not calling him to the kind of caring which would deplete his emotional resources further, so that there is nothing left for his family or for the next day's work. I believe that he is right to spend his evenings relaxing with his family and being refreshed and recreated for the next day's expenditure of himself. He is giving himself unstintingly to his work and cannot take on extra loads by caring for a lot of needy people. Here is a lesson for those of us who do too much, but not an excuse for those who tend to be lazy.

A mother talked to me about the role a single girl was

playing in her family. For years this young woman has been part of the household; she is known as 'aunty', she has a front door key, comes and goes as she pleases, and shares holidays with the family. A crisis cropped up unexpectedly when her presence started to be resented by a daughter in her early teens. When the daughter was four years old she loved to share a room with 'aunty'. Now she wants a room to herself. Anyway, daughter rather resents 'aunty's' intrusion into the family. The parents are perplexed, for the young woman is now part of their family lifestyle. They have forgotten that toddlers grow into teenagers who would often rather not have their parents in the house, let alone 'foreign' adults who invade the privacy of their rooms without their unqualified, unpressurised consent. A complicated situation arises. Mother dares not share the problem with the single woman in case she is hurt, and teenager now refuses to go on holiday with the family if 'aunty' is coming. The mother is trapped between the conflicting needs of two she loves. She knows her daughter requires a home as a refuge at this stage in her life. However, she knows that the young woman has recently lost her widowed father, and is vulnerable to any threat of rejection. She might be hurt if she were asked not to come round so often.

If only common sense could rise above heightened emotional tensions, and the mother and the young woman continue their friendship outside the family. Then by waiting for a few months or a few years the single woman could re-enter the family unit in the place that is uniquely hers.

To allow a single person to become part of the family is fraught with pain as much as joy on both sides.

A single person took the children from a family she knew on holiday and recalls, 'Perhaps it would be better to avoid such happy times. I am left afterwards with an intolerable sense of loss. We were surrounded by families of parents and children. The subtle, flattering temptation was for those few days to think of those children as "mine"; that our relationship was the same as that of other families around . . . I must admit to finding this experience (intimate involvement with several from the same family) extraordinarily disturbing. I was terrified at how powerful my affection for them was becoming, a protectiveness, which had I not seen the warning signs long in advance, would have turned into possessiveness.'

89

The parents of those children were delighted that all concerned had been so happy, and had no idea that their unmarried friend reacted, 'I am distrustful of such times of happiness – they always represent the good which will be snatched away as soon as one begins to enjoy it.'

Parents who gladly share their children with a single person need some kind of emotional antennae which will enable them to sense whether their children are helping or hindering at any one time. They need to know whether that single person is causing unhelpful and potentially harmful tension by being in the family at certain times.

Blessed is the family who had a relationship with a single person in which there is *mutual* sharing and caring. Blessed are those who can sit down as three adults and honestly share the dynamics of the family as they understand it at the moment in which they are talking, and who recognise that families change constantly as children pass through different stages of maturity. Doubly blessed is the family which is extended to include a single person in such harmony that these things are understood without discussion, in the knowledge that the love which unites them will prevent feelings from being hurt. Triply blessed is that family if the single person opts out temporarily or loosens ties, giving the family freedom to be alone more if it is sensed that the presence of a third adult may be a threat to the marriage, or may pose problems for the children, or is more than a nuclear family can cope with at that time – due to housing pressures for example, or tensions between growing children and their parents. Such a single person ultimately cannot but be more deeply rooted in the family by temporary absence than by awkward presence at the wrong time. Roots of real love sink deeper into the soil of such relationships.

I believe we have received more from single people who have opened themselves to us and cared for us than our family could ever have offered the unmarried friends who from time to time have been part of our lives.

I deeply empathise with the single girl who has said repeatedly of the family with whom she is friendly, 'Why do they always expect me to go to them? I have a flat and I can cook, and I want them to come and have a meal with me.'

Integration of singles and marrieds is not some kind of married couple corporation offering soup kitchen charity to needy singles. Far from it! Between the married couple and the single person must exist a relationship of mutual friendship so that neither side is ' being done good to'. If such a relationship exists then this feeling cannot enter in. Any suggestion by the married or the single of 'being an object of charity' is abhorrent.

A relationship problem can occur between a married couple and a single person if one of the three feels excluded. An intellectual man may have married a home-maker. A single woman may become part of the family, and imperceptibly the wife finds she is unable to enter into conversations between her husband and their friend. She cannot understand what they are talking about, if she comments she reveals her ignorance, and begins to feel inferior, and that her husband might prefer not to have married her. If all three involved can spot danger signs, and ease the friendship early, then a hurtful breaking off of relationships can be avoided. One can imagine many variations on this theme. If we truly care then all concerned must seek the highest good of the others, even when this involves loosing close, meaningful ties.

A single person can enhance life creatively for the children in a family. If that person can see the children as individuals and treat each as a person in his or her own right, then much can be done to make a child feel of significance.

I have heard children's pleased reactions, 'Aunty June treats us all differently. Do you remember, she took you bird-watching, she took me swimming and she took him to a film?'

The non-judgemental, accepting adult single person who is part of the family may turn out to be a helpful confidante and adviser to a teenager, which a parent often cannot be. A teenage daughter may find it far easier to pour out her boy-friend troubles to the elderly widow who comes to tea some Sundays, and obviously cares for each child, than she can to her parents (this is part of normal adolescent growing up and growing away from parental dependence; it is not because parents are failing as parents). In such ways the single friend in a family may contribute tremendously.

Tension arises when the care being given to others is such that children are feeling, or are being, neglected. If someone comes into a family situation and so monopolises everyone's time and resources that there is no time for the children, then a careful review must be made. Most families can cope in crises, but not with having their lives disrupted continually by the intrusion of others. The stability that is necessary for most people may lead to the drastic step of having to say, 'No' to someone in need, because it would adversely affect one or more members of the family.

I believe this is in keeping with the spirit behind the Bible words, 'If anyone does not provide for his relatives, and especially for his immediate family, he had denied the faith and is worse than an unbeliever' (1 Timothy 5:8).

We must remember that from a child's viewpoint, severe neglect may constitute failure to keep a promise to mend a broken toy, or take him to play football. We have effectively pushed him aside to tend to an adult's needs. He is too small and inarticulate to tell us how much he loves us, and longs for just a fraction of the attention we lavish on the adults who monopolise us – especially those who keep us for hours on the telephone in the precious play time that is his before bedtime. We could so easily take the coward's way out and fail to say, 'I'm not free to talk now, could you ring again in an hour?'

We may establish a pattern of pushing children aside, forgetting that they too are needy people. Our own families must have prior claim on our time and energy. As adults, we must leave room for *our* parents too. How hard we find it to sort out priorities!

We know we are to love but we have to learn to love so that others are not neglected. It is hard to remain calm and giving in the face of the many demands made on us. At such times we need to retreat with the words, 'Be still and know that I am God'. As we ask God he will show us his pattern for our priorities.

CHAPTER THIRTEEN

Costly caring

OVER the years in which I have learnt the lessons shared in this book I have become more deeply aware that Biblical commands like, 'Love your neighbour as yourself' and, 'carry each other's loads' may have meanings deeper than the obvious. It is easy for us to miss these insights.

My friend, Ly Lorn, who escaped from Cambodia in June 1979, obviously senses the deeper dimension which I find hard to define. I knew her for only three days in a refugee transit centre in Bangkok. Yet she and I were linked by a strong chain long before we met. She assisted me and translated for me, when I worked as a doctor there for three days. We had very few moments in which to speak to one another alone. Yet, she intuitively grasped and understood something about me which I never expressed in words to her. Her recognition and acceptance of a situation which I find hard to define makes me believe that I *have* stood on the brink of something greater than I had realised.

In November 1979 she writes from America:
'Dearest Doctor Anne, I have received your letter safely. It very wonderful to hear from you and show us that you love my people and thinking of them very much. I tell you the true dear, I can't find a word to say how I thank you God that brought us to America safely. We are love him and pray in his Name as our Saviour in our life. I read your letter and while I read it I cried because I miss you, and wanted to see you, and your family so. You are a very honest person I think. You know we just know each other for a short time in Thailand camp but I don't know why I love you like this. This is show us that God work in your heart and my heart, yes, dear I never forget to pray for you and your family.

'I have your photograph that you gave me when we were in camp. Sometime I miss you very much. I look in your

93

picture and make me happy on the time while I see you. Thank you, again for your letter which show us that you still remember both of us, and also show that you love my people, my relatives very much. Please pray for my people and asking God to forgive their sin. And asking him please continue to bring food, rice, medicine to help them to be safe and know him . . . '

As we enter into the spiritual dimensions of 'Bearing one another's burdens' we can do so at a deeper level than most of us comprehend. I was concerned about Cambodia for years; I was so concerned that I shared this with only my husband and one other friend. There was an element in my prayer for Cambodia in which it seemed as if I was weighed down by a heavy load. If my concern could ease the load crushing some Cambodians under the terrible Khmer Rouge regime then, I pledged before God, I was willing to carry that load. I began to understand a little more of what it meant to be part of Christ's body, the church and to suffer with Cambodians as they suffered. The radio news, and newspapers in Thailand kept me well informed of what was happening. These events which hit the Western mass media only at the end of 1979 were part of my daily life for five years.

Ly Lorn seemed to understand that there was an indefinable spiritual component about my love for Cambodia even though she and I met only in the clinic run by the Red Cross and spent our time treating the sick.

During the same period, another acquaintance shared problems with me. I cannot understand the mechanism of this, but I sensed that this person was different from others in my life. It was almost as if this individual had been given to me for the express purpose that for a short time I should learn what it meant to try to 'carry the load' of another human being. At some stage in our relationship I made a pact, 'You cannot do your important job if you are bearing all these burdens you have shared with me. So, if you want to hand them over in part, or completely, then I'll try to carry them for you.'

I had no idea at the beginning of this relationship, nor at the beginning of my involvement with Cambodia, the spiritual and emotional price that I was to pay for this offer of 'burden bearing'.

To attempt to stand in the shoes of another person and of

another race, to understand what was happening and then to bear a small part of the weight of pain was painful for me. The hurt of others hurt me. Yet this was something I had deliberately allowed, and understood to be something that God was asking of me.

In both cases I reached the point where I had to opt out, for I could not cope with the load indefinitely.

Interestingly enough, when I asked God to relieve me of the burden of Cambodia because it was crushing me emotionally, I was then asked to help Cambodia physically. Giving practical help costs very little more than physical exhaustion, giving up a few comforts, and being willing to free my husband from home ties so that he too could serve Cambodia's needs. Interestingly enough, this price was nothing to pay in comparison with the cost that spiritual 'burden bearing' had been to me.

I believe that God calls a few of us to enter into this deeper spiritual level of 'bearing one another's burdens'. I hope that I shall be strong enough, and willing enough to go through the hurt of this again if it is required of me.

When we are wanting God to love through us it is difficult to realise that we may be limited by our humanity. We may come to the point where we have to say, 'No' because we can no longer cope emotionally, spiritually or physically.

As I shared my reactions to events in South East Asia, this was one response; ' . . . One of the clues to the mystery of suffering is that it always constitutes and creates situations where something has to be done – which implies that suffering makes situations where something *can* be done. But even this is too easy. What *can* be done for the victims of Communism in Cambodia and Vietnam? Their plight is so much more plain in your letters and diaries than in the news, in the papers, or on the television. Somehow we have become insensate to the news on our media. Somehow you pierce beneath my thick skin. I feel so sick and sad about it all.'

We must learn to know ourselves and how much God wants us to enter into his work of caring for his world. Since none of us are sinless there are no easy guidelines to follow.

We face a dilemma. Jesus cared so much that he allowed himself to be crucified. He cared so much that he gave everything, even his life.

Here I believe we each face a problem we can resolve only

95

on our knees and nowhere else. We can either give ourselves totally to others so that in the face of their needs our resources are rapidly depleted. We will then presumably have a short life. Or we can try long term to work out a lifestyle which will enable us to serve most effectively for the longest possible time.

It may then appear to others that we sacrifice and care less than those who 'burn out for God'. We may face criticism for being 'half-hearted'.

This is not really a matter for discussion (beyond husband and wife) because it is something very private between us and God. If we determine to live as Jesus lived, and try to learn to love as he loved, then he alone can direct us to the manner in which we should live. No two people are alike. We tread a solitary path with no one to copy. We shall be criticised whichever choice we make (but let us never criticise another person).

Let us take a long solemn look at the cross where One cared beyond our capacity to care. As we gaze on the silent figure, let us solemnly seek to understand how we personally can love as he loved. We will never understand the mystery of suffering in our world but we *can* work to relieve such suffering.

We must get up from our knees and do something. We must act now before it is too late to help. Our lives may be half over, and those for whom we are to care may be beyond all help if we lazily put things off until time is more convenient.

The time will never be convenient, for caring is inconvenient.